Suzanne Collins

Other books in the People in the News series:

Maya Angelou	Ashton Kutcher
Tyra Banks	Taylor Lautner
Glenn Beck	Spike Lee
David Beckham	George Lopez
Beyoncé	Tobey Maguire
Sandra Bullock	Eli Manning
Fidel Castro	John McCain
Kelly Clarkson	Barack Obama
Hillary Clinton	Michelle Obama
Stephen Colbert	Apolo Anton Ohno
Miley Cyrus	Danica Patrick
Ellen Degeneres	Nancy Pelosi
Johnny Depp	Katy Perry
Leonardo DiCaprio	Tyler Perry
Hilary Duff	David Petraeus
Zac Efron	Queen Latifah
Brett Favre	Daniel Radcliffe
Roger Federer	Condoleezza Rice
50 Cent	Rihanna
Jeff Gordon	Alex Rodriguez
Al Gore	Derrick Rose
Tony Hawk	J.K. Rowling
Salma Hayek	Shakira
Jennifer Hudson	Tupac Shakur
LeBron James	Will Smith
Jay-Z	Gwen Stefani
Derek Jeter	Ben Stiller
Steve Jobs	Hilary Swank
Dwayne Johnson	Taylor Swift
Angelina Jolie	Justin Timberlake
Jonas Brothers	Usher
Elena Kagan	Lindsey Vonn
Alicia Keys	Denzel Washington
Kim Jong II	Serena Williams
Coretta Scott King	Oprah Winfrey

Suzanne Collins

By Elizabeth Hoover

LUCENT BOOKS
A part of Gale, Cengage Learning

GALE
CENGAGE Learning·

Detroit • New York • San Francisco • New Haven, Conn • Waterville, Maine • London

LIBRARY OF CONGRESS CATALOGING-IN-PUBLICATION DATA

Hoover, Elizabeth.
  Suzanne Collins / by Elizabeth Hoover.
    p. cm. -- (People in the news)
  Includes bibliographical references and index.
  ISBN 978-1-4205-0762-1 (hardcover)
1. Collins, Suzanne--Juvenile literature. 2. Authors, American--21st
century--Biography--Juvenile literature. 3. Women authors, American--21st
century--Biography--Juvenile literature. I. Title.
  PS3603.O4558Z685 2012
  813'.6--dc23
  [B]
                                                                2012005420

Lucent Books
27500 Drake Rd
Farmington Hills MI 48331

ISBN-13: 978-1-4205-0762-1
ISBN-10: 1-4205-0762-1

Printed in the United States of America
1 2 3 4 5 6 7 16 15 14 13 12

Contents

Fame and celebrity are alluring. People are drawn to those who walk in fame's spotlight, whether they are known for great accomplishments or for notorious deeds. The lives of the famous pique public interest and attract attention, perhaps because their experiences seem in some ways so different from, yet in other ways so similar to, our own.

Newspapers, magazines, and television regularly capitalize on this fascination with celebrity by running profiles of famous people. For example, television programs such as *Entertainment Tonight* devote all their programming to stories about entertainment and entertainers. Magazines such as *People* fill their pages with stories of the private lives of famous people. Even newspapers, newsmagazines, and television news frequently delve into the lives of well-known personalities. Despite the number of articles and programs, few provide more than a superficial glimpse at their subjects.

Lucent's People in the News series offers young readers a deeper look into the lives of today's newsmakers, the influences that have shaped them, and the impact they have had in their fields of endeavor and on other people's lives. The subjects of the series hail from many disciplines and walks of life. They include authors, musicians, athletes, political leaders, entertainers, entrepreneurs, and others who have made a mark on modern life and who, in many cases, will continue to do so for years to come.

These biographies are more than factual chronicles. Each book emphasizes the contributions, accomplishments, or deeds that have brought fame or notoriety to the individual and shows how that person has influenced modern life. Authors portray their subjects in a realistic, unsentimental light. For example, Bill Gates—the cofounder and former chief executive officer of the software giant Microsoft—has been instrumental in making personal computers the most vital tool of the modern age. Few dispute his business savvy, his perseverance, or his technical expertise, yet critics say he is ruthless in his dealings with competitors and driven more by his desire to maintain Microsoft's dominance in the computer industry than by an interest in furthering technology.

In these books, young readers will encounter inspiring stories about real people who achieved success despite enormous obstacles. Oprah Winfrey—one of the most powerful, most watched, and wealthiest women in television history—spent the first six years of her life in the care of her grandparents while her unwed mother sought work and a better life elsewhere. Her adolescence was colored by pregnancy at age fourteen, rape, and sexual abuse.

Each author documents and supports his or her work with an array of primary and secondary source quotations taken from diaries, letters, speeches, and interviews. All quotes are footnoted to show readers exactly how and where biographers derive their information and provide guidance for further research. The quotations enliven the text by giving readers eyewitness views of the life and accomplishments of each person covered in the People in the News series.

In addition, each book in the series includes photographs, annotated bibliographies, timelines, and comprehensive indexes. For both the casual reader and the student researcher, the People in the News series offers insight into the lives of today's newsmakers—people who shape the way we live, work, and play in the modern age.

The Thinking Kid's Best Seller

Writer Suzanne Collins was forty-six when she published *The Hunger Games*, a novel for young adults set in a dark future where North America has been obliterated by war and climate change. The residents of Collins's dystopia are forced to send their children to fight to the death in a sadistic game created by the government. The book wrestles with meaty themes: the effect of war, the dangers of voyeurism in popular culture, how governments use hunger and threats of violence to control populations.

Collins, who spent the first eighteen years of her writing career in television, had also taken on the theme of war and its costs in a well-received children's book series called The Underland Chronicles. She expected *The Hunger Games* would be another modest success, enough to allow her to continue her quiet lifestyle living in Connecticut with her family and beloved cats as she planned her next writing project.

Instead, *The Hunger Games* climbed to the top of the *New York Times* best-seller list and parked there for more than one hundred consecutive weeks. Fans—both teens, who were the book's intended audience, and adults, who enjoyed the action-packed novel's political message—eagerly awaited the second installment. By the third book, they were camping out in costume to be first in line to snag the novel at its midnight release. As of April 2012, an estimated 36.5 million copies of Collins's Hunger Games trilogy have sold. With the release of the *Hunger Games* movie in March 2012, sales figures were only expected to climb.

Thanks to the phenomenal success of her novels The Hunger Games, Catching Fire, *and* Mockingjay, *author Suzanne Collins was named to Time magazine's 2010 list of the "100 Most Influential People in the World."*

While Collins's trilogy is set to become an international multi-media phenomenon, the author is reluctant to step into the spotlight and guards her privacy carefully. She expects her celebrity to fade and concentrates instead on what matters most to her: writing for young adults and children so that they better understand the violence of the world around them. Her hope is that if children are exposed to the ethical and moral complexities of war they will grow up to be adults who desire to find nonviolent solutions to conflict.

A Question of Ethics

As the child of a military historian and U.S. Air Force officer, Collins was introduced to questions about the necessity of war from early childhood. Her father felt strongly about teaching his children about the history of warfare, and together they toured countless battlefields both in America and abroad. At the center of all his history lessons was the question: Given the cost of war, when is violence justifiable? Her father knew firsthand the devastating effects of war: He served in Vietnam for a year when Collins was just six and returned home plagued by nightmares. Growing up, Collins was regularly awakened by his screams.

Collins's experiences with her father transformed her into a writer deeply invested in writing about violence—not for entertainment but so that her readers can understand its true costs and ask themselves when it is appropriate to use force. "If we introduce kids to these ideas earlier, we could get a dialogue about war going earlier and possibly it would lead to more solutions," she posits. "I just feel it isn't discussed, not the way it should be. I think that's because it's uncomfortable for people. It's not pleasant to talk about. I know from my experience that we are quite capable of understanding things and processing them at an early age."[1]

And yet her novels avoid tedious moralizing or long-winded expositions. Instead readers are gripped by the trials and triumphs of Collins's compelling characters. Fans line up to find out what happened to sixteen-year-old Katniss Everdeen, the talented archer who captured readers' hearts when she volunteered to take her younger sister's place in the games. Rather than tell her readers about how committing acts of violence affects a person's mental state, she allows her readers to experience the nightmares of Peeta Mellark, the gentle baker's son who is torn apart by visions of the children he was forced to kill to survive the games. They watch Gale Hawthorn, Katniss's friend and hunting partner, turn into a calculating strategist for the rebellion.

Readers are also drawn into the love triangle between Katniss, Peeta, and Gale, but the choice Katniss struggles with is not between two boys but between two worldviews: one that is committed to nonviolence and the other that sees violence as justifiable if it is done in the name of a just cause. Yet Laura Miller, a critic for the *New Yorker*, points out, "*The Hunger Games* is not an argument. It operates like a fable or a myth, a story in which outlandish and extravagant figures and events serve as conduits for universal experiences."[2]

Mythical Inspiration for Contemporary Times

If *The Hunger Games* reads like a myth, as Miller says, it is because Collins found her inspiration in Greek mythology. She fell in love with these ancient tales when she was young, reading her mother's copy of *A Child's Book of Myths and Enchanted Tales*. One myth in particular—that of Theseus and the Minotaur—resonated with Collins because it showed how ruthless leaders keep their power by threatening the population and how one courageous person can stand up to a tyrant.

She also draws inspiration from the everyday. The story of *The Hunger Games* came to her as she was channel surfing between a reality television show and coverage of the Iraq war. She was struck by how the reality show mimicked the violence on the news coverage. She wondered: Could the viewer forget that the war was real and become desensitized to suffering and death?

In *The Hunger Games* she explores this question by taking it to its logical extreme: She creates a game that features real death as just a clever plot twist, but for the reader the death scenes are heart-wrenching. A reviewer for *Time* notes that Collins's books "expose children to exactly the kind of violence we usually shield them from. . . . They know all about violence and power and raw emotions. What's really scary is when adults pretend that such things don't exist."[3]

As much as Collins loved writing these novels and working on the films based on them, she is ready to move on to other projects. She continues, however, to be driven by the goals that sparked *The Hunger Games*: to inspire young readers to look critically at the world around them and ask how they might contribute to a more peaceful tomorrow.

Chapter 1

An Unsheltered Childhood

Suzanne Collins was born on August 11, 1962, to Michael and Jane Collins in New Jersey, the youngest of three girls and a boy. As a child, she moved constantly, every time her father, a U.S. Air Force officer, was reassigned. As a kid Suzanne enjoyed doing gymnastics and playing in the woods with her friends, but her childhood was far from carefree. From a young age, she was exposed to the reality, history, and moral complexities of war.

A Military Family

Suzanne was a member of a military family. Her grandfather served in World War I and her uncle in World War II. Even as a youngster she knew that her grandfather had been gassed and her uncle had survived shrapnel wounds. Her father, who was a scholar of military history with a doctorate in political science, often talked to his children about his profession.

Suzanne was familiar with military life and grew up mostly on air force bases. One of her earliest memories is watching young men in uniform perform drills at the U.S. Military Academy at West Point, New York, where her father briefly taught military history. The drills at West Point are large public events, with hundreds of spectators crowing into the stands to watch the young cadets march in lockstep while twirling rifles. The oldest continuously operated military post in the United States, West Point was an oversized classroom for Suzanne's father, who loved to point out historic buildings or show how its position above the Hudson River gave the Continental army (the American army that fought for independence against the British in the Revolutionary War) control of the waterways.

Waiting for Her Father's Return

In addition to hearing stories about war, Suzanne personally felt its painful effects when she was just six years old. In 1968, her father left to serve in the Vietnam War. While he was overseas, Jane moved the family to Indiana. What Suzanne remembers the most from that year was anxiously awaiting news of her dad. Because she was so young, she had trouble expressing her fears. "If your parent is deployed and you are that young, you spend the whole time wondering where they are and waiting for them to come home," she told a *New York Times* reporter many years later. "But you don't really have the words to express your concern."[4]

U.S. Marines fight in Vietnam during the Tet Offensive in 1968. Suzanne's father Michael Collins served in the military at the height of the war. His military experiences had great influence on Suzanne and her writing.

Vietnam in Pictures

Suzanne Collins's father fought in the Vietnam War, which began in November 1955 as a civil war between the North Vietnamese, supported by Communist allies, and the South Vietnamese, supported by the United States. The United States sent combat troops to aid the South Vietnamese from 1965 to 1973. Nearly sixty thousand American soldiers lost their lives in this conflict.

Television critic Michael Arlen dubbed Vietnam the first "living-room war."[1] It was the first time Americans could watch a conflict on their television sets at home. Perhaps one of the most famous images from 1968—the year Suzanne's father was deployed—was of a South Vietnamese police officer shooting a bound prisoner in the head at point blank range. The image caused "immediate revulsion at a seemingly gratuitous act … seen as emblematic of a seemingly gratuitous war."[2]

Other iconic images from that year include a February cover of *Life* magazine showing two soldiers slumped in a trench, faces swaddled in bloody bandages with the headline "The War Goes On;" a March cover of *Newsweek* depicting a huge explosion at an ammunition dump hit by a shell and marines running for cover; and police beating antiwar protesters at the 1968 Democratic Convention in Chicago.

1. Quoted in The Museum of Broadcast Communication. "Vietnam on Television." www.museum.tv/eotvsection.php?entrycode=vietnamonte.

2. Thomas, Robert McG., Jr. "Nguyen Nogc Loan, 67, Dies; Executed Viet Cong Prisoner." *New York Times*, July 16, 1998, p. A27.

The year of Michael Collins's deployment marked the peak of U.S. involvement in Vietnam. In January of that year, the nation was shocked when the North Vietnamese broke a truce normally held on the Vietnamese holiday of Tet (the lunar new year) and launched a widespread offensive, which included attacks on the U.S. embassy in Saigon. Meanwhile, there were antiwar protests across the nation, some of which turned violent. The year 1968 was also marked by the assassinations of two leaders: Martin Luther King Jr. and Robert Kennedy.

Suzanne's mother did her best to shield her children from the sometimes-graphic imagery that accompanied the news coverage of the year's events, but it was impossible. "Even though my mom tried to protect us . . . sometimes the TV would be on, and I would see footage from the war zone. I was little, but I would hear them say 'Vietnam,' and I knew my dad was there, and it was very frightening,"[5] she remembers. She also remembers, however, that her parents' willingness to speak openly with her about the war helped ease her fears.

The family joyously greeted Michael when he came home in 1969. Like many soldiers, he was deeply affected by what he experienced in combat. For the rest of his life he was plagued by nightmares of what he saw while overseas. Suzanne remembers being awakened by his screams in the middle of the night. Seeing the long-lasting psychological impact of war and violence left a deep impression on her.

History Lessons

Her father's trauma did not dampen his enthusiasm for military history, however. Five years after he returned, Michael, now a lieutenant colonel, accepted a position with the North Atlantic Treaty Organization (NATO), a group of allied countries from North America and Europe. The family moved to Brussels, Belgium. He loved to take eleven-year-old Suzanne and her siblings to historic battlefields, old forts, and imposing castles while regaling them with stories of the various wars fought throughout Belgium's history.

Suzanne remembers her years in Belgium as being a long but captivating history lesson. "It wasn't enough to visit a battlefield, we needed to know why the battle occurred, how it played out, and the consequences," she recalls. "Fortunately, he had a gift for presenting history as a fascinating story. He had a good sense of exactly how much a child could handle, which is quite a bit."[6] Her dad's lecturing not only taught her the history of European warfare but also how to tell a story about violence to children.

Often her dad's stories would completely transform Suzanne's perspective. For example, she remembers visiting castles that seemed to her to be "fairy-tale magical,"[7] but during the tour her father would pull her aside to show how the windows were angled so that archers could shoot arrows without being seen by the enemy and point out places where soldiers poured boiling oil down on attackers. These stories taught her about defensive tactics and also dispelled any ideas of fairy-tale castles and princesses that a teenage girl might have.

Her Father's Critical Influence

One particularly transformative experience came while Suzanne was admiring a poppy field near their house in Belgium. Looking out at the carpet of red flowers, she remembered a scene from the movie *The Wizard of Oz*, where Dorothy, the Scarecrow, Lion, and Tin Man run through a field of the flowers on their way to the magical Emerald City. When her father saw that same field, he thought of something very different—the graves of soldiers. He recited "In Flanders Field," a famous and moving World War I poem written by a Canadian lieutenant colonel named John McCrea after he watched his twenty-two-year-old friend killed on a battlefield. She remembers: "Boom! O.K. so this moment becomes transformative, because now I'm looking out onto that field and wondering if it was a graveyard."[8] For Michael, it was not enough to simply relate facts, dates, and numbers to his children. He also asked them to consider the ethical questions surrounding war and to reflect on its true costs; for example, "[At] the center of all this is the question of what makes a necessary war—at what point is it justifiable or unavoidable."[9]

Her father was influential not only because he provided Suzanne with an informal education in military history, but also because he possessed outdoor survival skills. He grew up during the Great Depression and learned to hunt wild animals and forage for edible plants as a way to supplement his family's meager food stores. As Suzanne notes, "For his family, hunting was not a sport but a way to put meat on the table."[10] As an adult, Michael often brought home game for dinner, but Suzanne's mother was cautious about the plants he found. Jane would not let her children eat what he had found, but Suzanne remembers watching him sauté and eat wild mushrooms with no ill effects.

A Love of Books

While her father turned the world into a classroom, Suzanne also found a rich world in the pages of her favorite books. Both her parents loved and encouraged reading. She also remembers an important English teacher, Mrs. Vance, who taught her in the fifth and sixth grades. Mrs. Vance would read Edgar Allan Poe stories to Suzanne's class on rainy days. Poe, an American writer who lived in the first half of the nineteenth century, is considered a master of the Gothic style, a type of writing that combines horror with romance.

Suzanne remembers hearing two specific stories by Poe. The first, "The Tell-Tale Heart," is told from the point of view of a murderer who dismembers his victim and hides the body parts beneath his floorboards. He thinks he can still hear his victim's heart beating under his floor and is slowly driven mad. The other, "The Masque of the Red Death," is about a prince who tries to hide from a plague by sequestering himself and his friends in his castle. One night they are having a masquerade ball, and a stranger enters the castle. The prince and his guests all die. Although some might find those stories too gory for a young audience, Suzanne remembers the class sitting "wide-eyed" and "riveted." She adds, "[Mrs. Vance] didn't think we were too young to hear it. . . . That made a huge impression on me."[11]

Another book Suzanne read in middle school that left a big impression on her was *A Wrinkle in Time* by Madeline L'Engle. This work of science fiction opens with a teenage girl named Meg wondering about her missing father, a subject that hit close to home for Suzanne. Meg goes on a quest to find him and, with the help of mysterious guides, visits various planets. L'Engle makes each planet a distinct world, with its own race of beings, government structure, and landscape. Suzanne was also taken with

The main character of Edgar Allan Poe's "The Tell-Tale Heart," a murderer, is driven mad. As a child, Suzanne loved to read. She remembers this Edgar Allan Poe story capturing her imagination.

Some of Suzanne's Favorite Books

Suzanne Collins was an avid reader as a child and young adult. One of her favorite books was *A Tree Grows in Brooklyn* by Betty Smith. Set in the first two decades of the twentieth century, this book tells the story of an impoverished Irish American family in Brooklyn. It addresses class inequity, gender roles, and violence against women.

She also loved *The Heart Is a Lonely Hunter* by Carson McCullers. This 1940 novel takes place in a mill town in Georgia and tells the story of John Singer, a deaf mute, and the people who know him. McCullers sensitively portrays the lives of outsiders and how difference can create isolation.

While Smith and McCullers wrote realistic novels with straightforward plotting, Kurt Vonnegut wrote the disjointed and surreal *Slaughterhouse-Five*, another of Suzanne's favorites. It tells the story of an American prisoner of war who believes he can time travel while being held by the Germans in an underground slaughterhouse. She also enjoyed *Lord of the Flies* by William Golding, and *Boris* by Jaap ter Haar.

a book that belonged to her mother, *A Child's Book of Myths and Enchanted Tales* by Margaret Evans Price. In this collection, Price relates Greek and Roman myths, including the story of a king who required the people of Athens to send their children into a labyrinth to be killed and eaten by a monster that was half man and half bull. "Even as a kid, I could appreciate how ruthless this was,"[12] Suzanne recalls.

As she got older, Suzanne found herself gravitating to books like *Anna Karenina* by Leo Tolstoy and *Nineteen Eighty-Four* by George Orwell that dealt explicitly with social themes. These authors were inspired by contemporary issues—poverty, oppression, war, and racism—but rather than preaching about these, they instead explored them through the lens of compelling fictional characters.

A Flair for the Dramatic

Becoming a writer might seem like a natural choice for someone who grew up with a storytelling dad and a love of reading; however, at age twelve, Suzanne declared she wanted to be an actor, a decision her parents encouraged. "My parents were wonderful," she says. "They were always supportive about me being in the arts and that's a huge thing."[13] Suzanne acted in school plays, something she greatly enjoyed.

In addition to acting, Suzanne liked to learn languages. She attended an American school on the air force base, but living in a bilingual country—in Belgium people speak both French and Flemish—she had the opportunity to learn both of these languages. She and her brother would practice French together, often acting out the dialogues in their language workbooks.

For her last two years of high school, Suzanne returned to the United States. After graduation, she attended Indiana University (IU) in Bloomington, Indiana. Here, Suzanne jumped right into acting. During her first semester, in October 1980, she had a

As a teenager Suzanne Collins was passionate about acting, and performed in many school plays. It was not until her college years that she became fascinated with writing.

substantial part in *The Prime of Miss Jean Brodie*, a play about an unconventional teacher at a girl's school in Scotland.

At IU, Suzanne also started dating Cap Pryor, a young man from North Webster, Indiana, who shared her passion for performing. In high school he toured with "God's Children," a youth group from the Methodist Church who traveled the country singing Christian songs. They even recorded three albums.

While at IU, Suzanne was exposed to a range of plays. These included the more traditional dramas Cap acted in at the Brown County Playhouse as well as the cutting-edge modern works both of them appeared in at T300, the school's theater. In her junior year, she and Cap acted together in a violent thriller written by a graduate student called "Forest Games." The *Indiana Daily Student* called Cap's performance a "tour de force" and added that Collins gives an "equally good, restrained performance."[14]

However, Suzanne discovered another interest in her sophomore year: writing. "I didn't just want to speak the words on stage, I wanted to write them,"[15] she explains. At age twenty, she wrote her first one act play and fell in love with writing. While Cap continued to act in student productions, Suzanne concentrated on her dramatic writing.

Both she and Cap earned bachelor of arts degrees in theater and drama and telecommunications, a degree that prepared them for work in television. Suzanne finished her required courses in 1985, but she decided to continue attending classes until 1986. Finished with school and having found her true calling as a writer, Collins was ready to dive into writing in one of the most exciting places for theater: New York City.

Chapter 2

From the Stage to the Small Screen

Suzanne Collins had fallen in love with writing in college and knew she wanted to be a scriptwriter. Just as her parents had encouraged her desire to become an actress, they supported her decision to pursue writing. "They always allowed me to believe it was a possibility to be a writer as my profession," Collins says. "It wasn't just something other people did…. They encouraged me to follow that dream."[16] Armed with the confidence that a writing career was within reach, Collins left Bloomington to attend New York University's Master of Fine Arts program in dramatic writing.

Writing for the Stage

When Collins arrived in New York in 1987, the city was in the throes of a drug epidemic, which fueled widespread homelessness and crime. It was a big transition from her small college town in southern Indiana. New York was home to a vibrant theater and writing community, however, and not just on Broadway. Dozens of small, independent theaters were springing up—and folding—in the area around New York University (NYU) known as the East Village.

Collins had enrolled in a rigorous and prestigious program. NYU's Dramatic Writing Department is part of their renowned Tisch School of the Arts, the alma mater of dozens of famous

After earning a bachelor's degree from Indiana University, Collins spent two years at New York University enrolled in its prestigious dramatic writing program.

Dramatic Structure

While at New York University, Collins perfected her understanding of dramatic structure. Dramatic structure is how the action of a dramatic work such as a play or film is constructed. Learning this structure helped Collins understand how to write a well-plotted story.

Dramatic structure is based on the guidelines given by ancient Greek philosopher Aristotle, who wrote in his *Poetics*, "A whole is that which has a beginning, middle, and end." That statement forms the basis for the construction of a three-act play. Act I contains the exposition, or introduces the setting, the characters, their relationships, and the conflict. Act II contains the rising action. In other words, Act II is when the plot thickens, and characters start to make decisions that will lead them to greater conflict. Usually Act II also contains the turning point, which is when the conflict reaches its height and circumstances change for the main characters. Finally, Act III is the denouement, or resolution, when the conflict ends.

Aristotle. *Poetics.* Project Gutenberg. www.gutenberg.org/ebooks/1974.

actors, directors, and screenwriters. Director Martin Scorsese, actress Angelina Jolie, and playwright Tony Kushner all attended the school. During her two years at NYU, Collins worked intensively on her writing in small workshops led by professional writers and was required to create several finished works for both stage and screen.

At NYU, Collins honed her skills in writing dialogue, creating plots, and structuring a story. She learned the economy of language that is the hallmark of a good dramatist. While novelists describe the story's setting or narrate what is going on in a character's head, playwrights must focus on action. "Scripts are essentially dialogue and stage directions," Collins says. "And then you rely on your director, actors, and designers to bring so much physical and emotional detail to the story."[17]

Breaking In

One of Collins's first jobs in New York was at the Classic Stage Company. This respected off-Broadway theater company in Union Square "re-imagines" classics for contemporary audiences, staging "plays from the past that speak directly to the issues of today."[18] Founded in 1967, it is one of New York's oldest and most prestigious off-Broadway theaters. The year that Collins arrived in New York, Carey Perloff took over as artistic director of the Classic Stage Company. She wanted to take the company in a new direction. In addition to producing the mainstays of classic theater, Perloff added works by twentieth-century playwrights to the company's repertoire.

During her time at the Classic Stage Company, Collins had the opportunity to work not only on Shakespeare's classics, but also on the plays of experimental twentieth-century writers, including the Irish writer Samuel Beckett. In addition, she learned how various playwrights transformed novels into plays. She remembers reading several stage adaptations of *The Idiot*, a novel by nineteenth-century Russian writer Fyodor Dostoyevsky. It helped her consider multiple ways of condensing a work of fiction into a play and compare which scenes each adapter considered crucial to the story's development.

While Collins pursued her dream of being a writer, Cap Pryor continued to further his career as an actor. After earning his master of fine arts degree at Penn State University, he also moved to New York, and the two were soon married. The couple struggled to make it in the city's competitive theater scene. Pryor secured smaller parts in several off-off-Broadway plays. In 1991, he acted in the Triangle Theater Company's production of *Unchanging Love*, an adaptation of a short story by Russian writer Anton Chekhov. Even though it was performed in a small church, the production warranted a review in the *New York Times*.

A year later, Pryor joined the Synchronicity Theater Group (STG) as a founding member. The theater was on Mercer Street in SoHo, a neighborhood named after its location (south of Houston Street) that was home to a burgeoning arts scene. Pryor served as STG's producing director until 1998, when the company went out of business after being forced out of their space after rent skyrocketed as more wealthy people moved to trendy SoHo.

Breaking New Ground with *Clarissa*

During the 1990s, Pryor continued to work with the struggling STG, while Collins started writing for children's television. She joined teams of writers who worked on shows for Nickelodeon and Nick Jr. Even though Collins went from working on avant-garde theater to writing scripts about teenage girls or talking

Melissa Joan Hart played Clarissa in the Nickelodeon television show Clarissa Explains It All. *Collins began writing for the show in th 1990s.*

bears, she found the process to be basically the same. "I find there isn't a great deal of difference technically in how you approach a story, no matter what age it's for," she says. "The same rules of plot, character, and theme apply. You just set up a world and try to remain true to it."[19]

In 1993, Collins earned her first script credit, meaning she was listed in the show's credits. It was for an episode of Nickelodeon's *Clarissa Explains It All*, a sitcom that featured a teenage girl who spoke directly to the camera, "explaining" what was going on in the story. The hugely successful show was popular with both boys and girls, and "disproved the notion that boys would not watch shows starring girls,"[20] according to *New York Times* television writer Lisanne Renner. The show aired from 1991 to 1994 and in its final year was nominated for the Emmy for Outstanding Children's Program. *Clarissa's* success inspired a number of shows for teenagers featuring female leads.

Collins's first credit was for an episode that aired in season three. It centered on Sam, Clarissa's best friend, setting he and Clarissa up on a double blind date. Clarissa spends most of the show imagining all the ways the date could go wrong. Sam and Clarissa's friendship was another innovative aspect of the show. It was rare to see an onscreen friendship (not a romance) between a boy and a girl. Collins was also listed as a writer on an episode titled "A Little Romance." In this episode, Sam tries—and fails—to start a romance with Clarissa. In the end he realizes they are better off as friends.

Writing with a Team

For both episodes of *Clarissa*, Collins shared writing credits and duties with three or four other writers. But she was not worried about not having the spotlight to herself. In fact, she loved the collaborative nature of writing for television. "It can be really fun,"[21] Collins says about the process of working with other writers on a script. The writers' room on an innovative show like *Clarissa* must have been an exciting place for someone like Collins, who had a nuanced understanding of scriptwriting from her time in theater.

During the 1990s, writers were enjoying great appreciation for their contributions to television. The medium was changing; standard sitcoms that told stories in a straightforward manner gave way to shows with complex and interwoven plotlines. The writers led this transformation. In a 1997 article about television writing, James Sterngold explains, "It helps, too, ... that television shows are run by writers rather than deal makers. This produces a work environment that many regard as more intellectual and more in touch with the craft than [in] film."[22]

But television work meant more than fun and intellectual stimulation. It could also mean a seriously good paycheck. During the mid- to late 1990s, even a junior television writer could net more in a year than a young lawyer. Some writers earned around $5,000 an episode. In a twenty-two-episode season, even a writer just out of a college could earn $110,000. This was a good thing for Collins, as she and Pryor were just starting a family. In 1994, she gave birth to her first child, a son named Charlie.

From Staff Writer to Story Editor

An experienced scriptwriter, Collins left *Clarissa* and joined the writing team behind Nickelodeon's *The Mystery Files of Shelby Woo*. She became the show's story editor in 1997. As story editor, Collins was responsible for supervising a team of writers, editing scripts, and developing storylines.

Collins was again working on a show that broke new ground in terms of its casting; *Shelby Woo* the first popular show with a main character who was Asian. It was about a teenage girl who lives with her grandfather, an innkeeper, and works as an intern at the local police station. As an intern, Shelby is supposed to stick to administrative tasks, but she is always jumping in and solving the police officers' cases for them.

The show was an immediate success, netting a million viewers per episode in its first season. For the second season, the network decided to move the show to a higher-profile time slot. The show's producer, Alan Goodman, decided to revisit the scripts the team had already prepared to make the show more complex.

Cap on TV

While Collins was breaking into television as a writer, Pryor secured several roles acting on television shows and made-for-TV movies. The year before Collins began writing for *The Mystery Files of Shelby Woo*, Pryor played a part on one of the shows. In an episode titled "The Missing Dolphin," he portrayed an affable, if nerdy, boat repairman working for a marine lab. By the end of the episode, it is revealed he is actually the head of a smuggling ring. He also appeared in a 1992 TV movie *The Last P.O.W.? The Bobby Garwood Story*. The film was based on the true story of a U.S. Marine who claims he was a prisoner of the North Vietnamese Army for fourteen years. Pryor had a small part as a member of the aid organization the Red Cross.

"We didn't know our time slot was changing when we wrote these scripts, but now we'll be exposed to a wider audience and they'll be seeing a more adventurous show,"[23] he announced. Collins, who joined the show for its second season, was on the writing team tasked with making that happen. She stayed with the show through its successful 1998 season, helping create complex mysteries that kept viewers guessing.

The Seed Is Planted

In 2000, Collins gave birth to her second child, a daughter named Isabel. Shortly after that she began working on a television show called *Generation O!* This animated series aired in the United States on the WB Network and was about an eight-year-old rock star named Molly O. Children's book author and illustrator James Proimos helped create the show and the animation was based on his unique style.

Collins and Proimos worked closely together. As they collaborated, they became friends. One day, Proimos suggested that Collins write a children's book. "She seemed like a book writer to me," remembers Proimos. "She also had the style and the mind of a novelist. I was telling her that you can't do TV forever; it's a young person's business. With books, at the very worst, you start out slow, but you can do them for the rest of your life."[24]

Collins, however, wasn't interested. "I was like yeah, yeah, whatever,"[25] she recalls. She was still dedicated to screenwriting and worked hard to perfect her craft. She remembers that she once rewrote a script fourteen times before finally realizing she had to let it go and move on.

Sticking to Screenwriting

One of the reasons Collins dismissed Proimos's suggestion was that there was no reason for her to consider a change of career. After all, she was a very successful screenwriter who worked on popular and respected television series. In 2001, she cowrote the script for a critically acclaimed Christmas special called *Santa Baby!* This special was created by Rankin/Bass Productions, Inc., which was responsible for many beloved animated holiday specials in the 1960s and 1970s.

Rankin/Bass had not made a holiday special in sixteen years when it decided to produce *Santa Baby!* The episode centered on the 1953 hit song of the same name sung by Eartha Kitt. Yet again, Collins found herself working on a show that challenged assumptions about what kinds of characters audiences were interested in. The special aired on Fox and was one of the first Christmas specials meant for a wide audience that featured African American characters. The script, which Collins cowrote with Peter Bakalian, tells the story of a down-on-his-luck songwriter who finds work as a street Santa. His daughter's Christmas wish helps him out of his slump.

The show was peppered with hip-hop, jazz, and pop songs sung by musical superstars Patti LaBelle, Vanessa Williams,

Actress and singer Eartha Kitt performs on stage. Collins continued to write for TV, including a Christmas special called Santa Baby! The title referred to a 1953 hit song made popular by Kitt, who also voiced a part in the special.

and Kitt. Audiences were wowed by the still-powerful voice of Kitt, who was in her mid-seventies at the time. It was Collins's and Bakalian's writing, however, that caught the attention of the Writers Guild of America. The guild nominated them for an Outstanding Achievement Award. Although they did not win, the nomination was an important recognition from their colleagues.

Books for City Kids

In the eighteen years Collins wrote for children's television, she penned scripts not only for *Clarissa Explains it All, The Mystery Files of Shelby Woo,* and *Generation O!,* but also for *Little Bear* and *Oswald,* two animated series on Nick Jr. She eventually became the head writer for Scholastic Entertainment's *Clifford's Puppy Days* on the Public Broadcasting Service (PBS).

Though she showed no sign of wanting to leave TV writing, Collins continued to be pestered by Proimos to write a book. Meanwhile Pryor and Collins were raising two young children in the crowded, fast-paced, and relentlessly urban New York City. One day, Collins was reading one of her favorite books, Lewis Carroll's *Alice's Adventures in Wonderland.* This book, published in 1865, tells the story of a young girl who gets bored picnicking on the riverbank with her sister. To amuse herself, she runs after an unusual white rabbit and falls down a rabbit hole into a magical world populated by various talking animals and strange creatures, a baby that turns into a pig, and a royal court of playing cards.

While reading about Alice, Collins was struck by how many children's books were set in the countryside. What about books for Isabel and Charlie who rode the subway, lived in a city of more than 8 million people, and had to go to Central Park to see anything resembling Carroll's world? As Collins's website notes, "In New York City, you're much more likely to fall down a manhole than a rabbit hole and, if you do, you're not going to find a tea party."[26]

Collins became intrigued by the question of what someone would find. She did not yet know, but Proimos kept after her to write a book. "Finally I broke down and gave it a try,"[27] Collins says. With their young family squeezed for space, Collins and Pryor took the opportunity presented by her career change to move to nearby Connecticut, which is significantly less crowded than the areas just around New York City. There, at thirty-eight years old, Collins set out to write her first novel. But she needed help, so she called the person she knew could tell a compelling story: her father.

Chapter 3

The World Below

Once settled in Sandy Hook, Connecticut, with her family, Suzanne Collins began work on her first children's book, *Gregor the Overlander*. Taking her cue from Lewis Carroll's *Alice's Adventures in Wonderland*, Collins opens her novel with her protagonist falling through a portal into a magical underground world—except that Gregor does not start his day picnicking by a river and chasing rabbits. He is in the laundry room of his huge New York apartment building babysitting his two-year-old sister. And once down the portal, he does not find a tea party. Instead he finds a violent kingdom where humans battle giant rats for territory and resources.

Working with Dad

Collins knew her battle scenes needed to be compelling and the alliances between the different underground creatures had to be logical. She therefore decided to call someone who knew military history and strategy front-to-back: her dad. The two of them spent hours talking on the phone figuring out how the rats, cockroaches, spiders, and humans would ally themselves. The book also features scenes of soldiers training for battle, characters discussing military tactics, and summit meetings where alliances are negotiated.

A story about talking cockroaches and wisecracking rats may seems fantastical, but much of the book is grounded in what Collins learned about the military from her father. For example, after his fall, Gregor is taken to Regalia, a city where humans

When Collins switched from television writing to writing children's books, she wanted to engage her young readers in a story with an urban setting rather than one set in the rural countryside.

dwell. At the center of the city is an enormous castle. Much like the Belgian castle Collins visited as a teenager, the Regalian looks like it might be from a fairy tale, but it is also a perfectly designed fortress meant to repel enemy attacks. Gregor is ushered into a huge arena where the Regalians are doing drills, much like the West Point students Collins watched as a child—except the Regalians drill and fight on the backs of giant bats.

In the arena, Gregor meets Luxa, the stubborn young queen of Regalia and a skilled fighter. Luxa's two grandparents—Vickus and Solovet—represent two sides of military strategy. While Solovet leads the army and considers how to form efficient, deadly attacks, Vickus considers how alliances and concessions could help avoid those battles. These two are constantly debating a question familiar to Collins from her childhood: when is violence justifiable?

Unfortunately, Collins's father died before the book was published. While he never read the final book, his presence permeates the pages. In the opening scenes, Gregor is at home in his apartment waiting for his missing father to return, just as Collins waited for her own father to return from Vietnam. When Gregor is reunited with his dad, the reader meets a learned teacher who knows how to fashion a compass with a needle and a bit of cloth. Although Collins has never publicly said so, Gregor's father bears a strong resemblance to her own.

Home Alone

While she relied on conversations with her father to help her understand military strategy, Collins also did research on her own. She read through heaps of books on rats, bats, and cockroaches so she could realistically describe the creatures that populated the Underland. Reading and writing by herself was a new experience for Collins. She was used to the raucous conversations and creative exchange in the writers' rooms of television shows.

Collins quickly found she liked not only the quiet but also the fact that she could spend the day in her pajamas. She developed— and maintained—her own schedule of starting work right after breakfast, before distractions set in, and writing straight through until around three in the afternoon. In addition to enjoying her new routine she also discovered a sense of creative autonomy and freedom. "It's very refreshing to conceive of an idea and carry it through the whole process yourself," she said. "You get to hang on to your vision in a different way."[28]

Collins also liked the way in which working on a novel allowed her to create everything from scratch. When she worked on a TV script she had to conform to the rules of the already established setting and characters. In her novel, however, she created those rules. "I liked the fact that this world was teeming under New York City and nobody was aware of it," Collins says. "That you

The Dramatic Question

While writing her first novel, Collins used dramatic writing concepts to create a well-paced and suspenseful story. Collins says one of the ways she stays focused in her writing is to always keep in mind the dramatic question. The *dramatic question* is another term from scriptwriting. It is the question that arises after the turning point of the story and is always framed in terms of the protagonist's actions. For example, in *Gregor the Overlander* the dramatic question is: Will Gregor rescue his father from the rats?

could be going along preoccupied with your own problems and then whoosh! You take a wrong turn in your laundry room and suddenly a giant cockroach is right in your face. No magic, no space or time travel, there's just a ticket to another world behind your clothes dryer."[29]

Using her Background as a Scriptwriter

While Collins relished her quiet days dreaming up the Underland in her pajamas, other aspects of the transition from scriptwriter to novelist were harder. Her training in dramatic writing at NYU schooled her in penning dialogue and creating action—skills she perfected as a writer for television. But neither experience taught her how to describe a city or explain what it feels like to miss your mom or watch a friend die.

In an interview with *School Library Journal*, Collins discusses how she struggled through certain passages that describe the setting or mood: "I'd be clicking along through dialogue and action sequences. That's fine, that's like stage directions. But whenever I hit a descriptive passage, it was like running into a wall,"[30] she explains.

Sometimes it would take her hours to pen a single paragraph, a process she found exhausting. When it came to writing description, her background as a screenwriter was a handicap, but that background also helped her write a compelling and fast-paced narrative.

Her background in dramatic writing also helped her figure out how to structure her novel. Collins organized *Gregor the Overlander*—and all her following books—like a three-act play, only longer. They have twenty-seven chapters, broken into three parts of nine chapters each. "At the end of each 9 chapters a new part begins and I call each of those breaks 'act breaks' as you would in playwriting because that's how I think of them,"[31] Collins explains.

The Path to Publication

After six months of writing, Collins had a draft of *Gregor the Overlander*. Now, she needed to find an agent to shop her book around to publishers. Proimos, who had urged her to write a book in the first place, stepped in to help. He introduced her to his own agent, Rosemary Stimola, who specializes in representing authors of books for children and young adults.

Stimola knew right away that she wanted to be Collins's agent. "Quite honestly, I knew from the very first paragraph I had a very gifted writer," remembers Stimola. "She established a character I cared about. She established a story and a mood that touched my heart."[32] Stimola secured Collins a contract with Scholastic Books, where editor Kate Egan was in charge of seeing the book through to publication. Egan and Collins found they worked well with each other, and Collins enjoyed the editing process. In some ways it reminded her of collaborating on a television script.

The editing process began with Egan reading the manuscript, along with two other editors. Egan then compiled all their thoughts into a letter that offered suggestions and asked questions about overarching concerns, including character development and the story arc. Then Collins revised the manuscript, keeping their comments in mind. Egan read the new manuscript, making sentence-level changes and adding queries, or questions, in

Scholastic Books agreed to publish Collins's book Gregor the Overlander. *It was the first of many of her books that Scholastic would publish.*

the margins for Collins to answer. Finally a copyeditor combed through the manuscript fixing all grammatical errors and making sure the book read well.

The whole editing process can take several months, but finally the manuscript was ready to go to press. In 2003, when Collins was forty-one years old, Scholastic published *Gregor the Overlander*. Collins already knew she loved being a novelist, but now she was about to find out whether the public loved reading the book as much as she loved writing it.

Introducing Gregor to the World

Readers and critics alike embraced *Gregor*. *School Library Journal* lauded it as "an engrossing adventure,"[33] and *Publishers Weekly* added, "[Collins] does a grand job of world-building, with a fine economy of words—no unnecessary details bog down either the setting or the invigorating story."[34] The book became a *New York Times* best seller and won the New Atlantic Independent Booksellers Association Book of the Year Award.

While many reviewers praised the book for its thrilling action and finely rendered settings, others singled out the endearing protagonist. A reviewer for *Kirkus Reviews* wrote, "The abiding ache of Gregor's sadness is matched by his tender care for Boots [his younger sister]... . Wonderful."[35] Indeed, Gregor is an unlikely hero. Although he is called the Warrior in a strange Underland prophecy, he would rather not fight or kill anything. He is always trying to figure out ways to avoid confrontation. He is even compassionate toward the Crawlers, giant cockroaches that are much reviled in the Underland. When he discovers that he is a Rager, or a fighter of exceptional ability, he is sickened and embarrassed. In the first book, the only weapon he carries is a flashlight.

When Charlie McButton Lost Power

During the four years it took her to write the *Gregor* series, Collins also penned a book for younger readers (aged four and up) called *When Charlie McButton Lost Power*. The book is in rhyming verse. It tells the story of a boy named Charlie who is frantic because a power outage prevents him from playing his video games. He finds an old handheld game and steals batteries from his younger sister, Isabel. This behavior earns him a time-out, during which he begins to reflect on his behavior and decides that, instead of playing video games, he wants to try playing with his sister. The two children in the book—Charlie and Isabel—are named after, and perhaps based on, Collins's own children. The story was heralded as "lively" and praised for its "Seussian lilt," meaning it sounds like a Dr. Seuss book that makes it "perfect for reading outloud."

Laurie Slagenwhite. Review of *When Charlie McButton Lost Power*. *Library Media Connection*, April 2006, p. 60.

Collins freely admits that she shares some traits with her main character. In an interview with Scholastic editor Jen Rees, Collins remarks, "I think I'm like Gregor because we both want to do the right thing but sometimes have trouble figuring out what it is. Also, neither of us likes to ride roller coasters and we've both changed a lot of diapers."[36] Like Gregor, Collins confronted complex ethical issues surrounding violence and war when she was just a kid.

The Quiet Life

Gregor is not based entirely on his creator, however. Collins concedes that, unlike Gregor, she is terrified of rats and squeamish around cockroaches. She also claims to have a terrible sense of direction, while Gregor can find his way around the Underland in the dark. She tells Rees, "Cap [Pryor] says he would not take me to the Underland because I am not good in a emergency and I would constantly make him stop and ask for directions. Both of these things are true."[37]

Collins likes her quiet life in Connecticut, where the only bat she has to deal with is a large Balinese sculpture of a bat her husband bought her that hangs in their kitchen window. It is meant to be Ares, the large black bat that Gregor bonds to, or takes a pledge of mutual responsibility for the other's life. Collins says it is one of the best presents she has ever received. Sometimes they place stuffed rats and spiders on the sculpture, pretending he is giving them a ride.

Collins prefers to write about perilous journeys than to take them. Over the next four years, she did just that, writing four more books about Gregor's adventures in the Underland. Her sequels did not disappoint readers and were met with equal acclaim. According to Tasha Saecker in a review for *School Library Journal*, Collins "maintains the momentum, charm, and vivid settings of the original title"[38] in the books that follow. Despite the demands of writing five books in four years, Collins managed to also fit in a book for young readers called *When Charlie McButton Lost Power*. She also wrote for PBS's animated series *Clifford's Puppy Days*, a TV show about a giant red puppy.

The Dark Life of Gregor

In the sequels, Gregor confronts very dark—some would argue adult—themes. As the series progresses, the books explore increasingly disturbing territory. In *Gregor and the Marks of Secret*, for example, there are graphic depictions of the genocide of mice that harkens back to the Nazi Holocaust, the systematic, state-sponsored murder of 6 million Jews during World War II. In

In Gregor and the Marks of Secret, the second Gregor book in Collins's Underland series, the author explores darker topics, like a horrible genocide of mice.

Gregor and the Code of Claw, Gregor witnesses the horrific suffering of refugees from an enormous war. In each book, major characters perish in bloody scenes. A reviewer for *Kirkus Reviews* notes that *Gregor and the Curse of the Warmbloods,* the third volume in the series, "takes on an even darker tone than the earlier ones, delving into meaty questions of territorial expansion and its justification."[39]

Collins tries to prepare her young readers for the more violent passages in the writing that precedes them. "Kids will accept any number of things," she tells *Scholastic Instructor.* "I think somehow if you went on that journey with me from the beginning, you kind of worked into the more violent places and were prepared by what had come before."[40] Indeed, Collins seems to know instinctually what children can handle. In the *New York Times Book Review,* Gabrielle Zevin praised Collins for having "the light touch of a writer who truly understands writing for young people."[41]

Collins also relies on her own experience both as a daughter and as a parent to gauge what is appropriate for her readers. Her father seemed to know how much his children could handle when teaching them military history, so she uses those experiences as a barometer when considering just how graphically she should write. She also keeps her own children in mind. As she told Rick Margolis of *School Library Journal,* "I have two children of my own, so I can think about, 'Alright, how would I say this to them?'"[42]

War Stories?

By keeping in mind the age of her readers, Collins created a gripping narrative full of perilous journeys, terrifying duels, and suspenseful battles that are appropriate to her readership. Ultimately, the books are not just about the bloody details or the violent passages. Rather, they are also about how people deal with difficulty, forge friendships, and remain loyal in hard times. There is even a little romance thrown in.

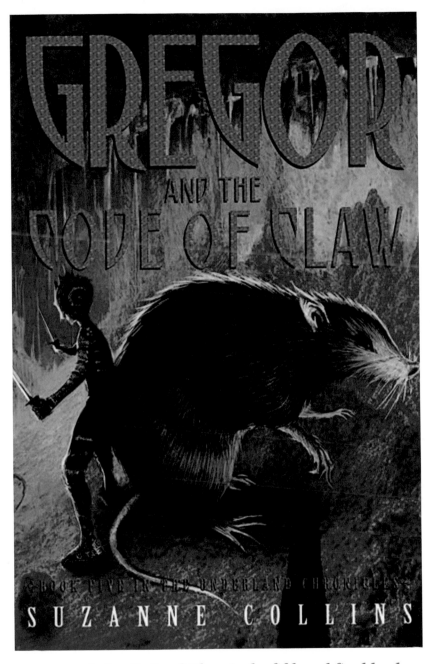

Gregor and the Code of Claw *is the fifth and final book in Collins's popular Underland Chronicles series.*

In writing about *Gregor and the Code of Claw*, the final book in the series, reviewer Kitty Flynn says, "Readers ... will be battle-weary but buoyed by Collins's ultimate message of hope."[43] In the end, Gregor, the so-called Warrior decides it is preferable to find a way of avoiding conflict through compromise. He muses on how to make the world a better place and concludes that that could only happen by "people rejecting war. Not one or two, but all of them. Saying it was an unacceptable way to solve their differences." But, he adds, "by the look of things, the human race had a lot of evolving to do before that happened."[44] Gregor's final thoughts suggest that Collins writes about violence not merely to entertain but rather to show war's true costs. She forces readers to ask questions about when it is right and ethical to use force, and in the final book she implies that the answer is almost never.

Like the authors she admired as a young adult, Collins's first series managed to transmit political and social messages without being preachy. The *Gregor* books helped her define herself as an author, one who uses compelling characters and suspense-ful plots to engage readers while tangling with larger themes of justice, violence, war, and peace. They also helped her make the transition from screenwriter to novelist. The Gregor series, however, while successful, did nothing to prepare her for the popularity of her next series.

Chapter 4

A Breakout Hit

The *Gregor* series proved Collins's mettle as a children's author. It also helped her net a six-figure deal with Scholastic for her next project: a trilogy set in a dystopian future. With Stephenie Meyer's *Twilight* series dominating young-adult fiction, sales expectations were modest for Collins's new book, *The Hunger Games*. But Collins was not thinking about sales—she was concerned with writing a socially relevant novel that would inspire young adults to reflect on the problems affecting the world around them.

Sylvester Stallone prepares to fight as the main character in the Rambo movies. Collins used these movies for reference when describing weapons in her books.

An Unlikely Source of Inspiration

One night Collins was channel surfing, switching between coverage of the Iraq war and a reality television show in which young people were pitted against each other. "I was tired, and the lines began to blur in this very unsettling way, and I thought of this story,"[45] she remembers. The story she came up with is set in a dark future in which North America has been destroyed by war and climate change. What is left of the country has been divided into twelve districts ruled by a tyrannical government located in the Capitol. Every year, each district must send one boy and one girl (called tributes) to fight to the death in the televised Hunger Games.

The games' designers try to maximize drama to entertain people in the Capitol. They might create a forest fire to drive the tributes together into a fight, or release vicious creatures to tear players to shreds. Collins drew on her experience in television to develop how the games' creators thought. "The crew who create the Hunger Games each year ... come from my work in television," she explains. "In a way, it's very easy for me to imagine the world of the gamemakers because, in a much gentler way, I was one myself."[46]

Writing about plucky teen detectives or talking puppies is "much gentler" than the brutal thinking of the gamemakers in *The Hunger Games*, so Collins did additional research to make these violent game realistic. She read a stack of books on survival skills and watched violent action movies. In particular, she relied on the *Rambo* films to help her accurately describe various weapons. The four-part series stars Sylvester Stallone as a troubled Vietnam veteran who is skilled not only with guns but also with a bow and arrow and his trademark hunting knife, as well as in hand-to-hand combat.

Classical Roots

While the initial inspiration came from today's television landscape, Collins also looked to the ancient past to help her fill out the plot. One major source of inspiration was the story of Theseus and the Minotaur, one of the stories in *A Child's Book of Myths and*

THESEVS SLAYS THE MINOTAVR

*Theseus kills the minotaur in a mythological story that captured Collins's imagination in childhood. The idea followed her into adulthood, and Collins used it as inspiration for the world she created in **The Hunger Games**.*

Enchanted Tales, the book that so captivated Collins as a girl. In this story, a sadistic king requires the people of Athens to send seven boys and seven girls to be thrown into a labyrinth and eaten by a vicious beast called the Minotaur. Prince Theseus finds a way to defeat the beast and save the other children. Collins saw this myth as a story of how the king used the labyrinth to keep the people in line. "[He] was sending a very clear message: 'Mess with us and we'll do something worse than kill you. We'll kill your children,'"[47] Collins explains. Like the king in the myth, the president in *The Hunger Games* requires the people of the districts to sacrifice their children as a way of demonstrating his absolute power.

Collins did more than update the story of Theseus to incorporate reality television. She also used her knowledge of history to

Theseus and the Minotaur

Collins based the idea of the Hunger Games on the Greek myth of Theseus and the Minotaur. This story begins with the king of Minos, Androgeos, laying siege to Athens to avenge his father's death. In return for stopping the siege, the Athenians agree that every nine years they will give Androgeos seven boys and seven girls to throw in a labyrinth with the Minotaur, a carnivorous monster who is half man and half bull. Collins argues that Androgeos does this to "remind [the Athenians] of their subjugation."

When it is time to send the children to Minos, the Athenian prince Theseus agrees to take the place of one of the boys. When Theseus and the children arrive at Androgeos's palace, the king tells them to enjoy themselves because tomorrow they will be sent to the labyrinth. During the evening's festivities the king's daughters both fall in love with Theseus and decide to help him. One gives him a ball of thread so he can find his way out of the labyrinth, and the other gives him a sword. The next day, Theseus slays the Minotaur and with the help of the thread to find their way back to the entrance of the labyrinth, leads the children to safety and back to Athens.

Quoted in James Blasingame. "An Interview with Suzanne Collins." *Journal of Adolescent & Adult Literacy,* May 2009, p. 727.

draw a parallel between the excesses of the ancient Roman Empire (27 BC–AD 476) and the materialism of contemporary celebrity culture. Toward the end of the Roman Empire, its territorial reach was almost too large to be governable. Internal political strife threatened to pull the empire apart. The rulers developed a strategy called *panem et circenses* or "bread and circuses," meaning they provided free wheat and lavish entertainment spectacles to gain and pacify their followers. The circuses featured gladiator games, where men (and sometimes women) engaged in armed combat with each other, wild animals, or condemned criminals to entertain the audience with bloodshed. Often the games' sponsor would decide whether the game should end with the defeated being carted off for medical care or skewered by his or her opponent. Collins alludes to the concept of "bread and circuses" in *The Hunger Games* by calling the country that has been cobbled together from the ashes of North America "Panem."

In order to create the games, Collins combines the story of Theseus with her knowledge of the gladiator games. As she tells Rick Margolis of *School Library Journal*, "[The main character, Katniss,] is a futuristic Theseus. But I didn't want to do a labyrinth story. So I decided to write basically an updated version of the Roman gladiator games."[48] In addition to drawing on her own knowledge of Roman history, Collins looked to Stanley Kubrick's classic 1960 film *Spartacus*. This three-hour epic set in ancient Rome tells the story of a slave who is trained to be a gladiator and uses this position and the skills he has learned to lead an uprising.

Another Memorable Character

While Collins's protagonist has aspects of Theseus and Spartacus in her personality, she is more than just a composite—she is a unique and compelling character. Sixteen-year-old Katniss Everdeen lives in District 12 and is an expert hunter who poaches game to feed her family. She is self-reliant, strong, and possesses a growing awareness of the injustices of the Capitol. Shortly after the book opens, readers learn that Katniss's father has died in a mining accident but that he has passed on his knowledge of

*The main character in **The Hunger Games** is a teenage girl named Katniss. Her father taught her to hunt and gather, skills that Collins learned from her own father.*

hunting to his daughter. Collins's childhood memories of her father hunting and gathering plants thus made their way into the books. Katniss's mother is a healer who uses medicinal plants to help the residents of District 12 who cannot afford medical care. Like Gregor, Katniss's character is defined by her loyalty to her younger sister, Prim. When her sister's name is called to be a tribute in the Hunger Games, Katniss steps forward to volunteer to take her place.

Collins planned to write the book in third person and past tense, just like the Gregor series. But as she was writing, she says, "the words just came out, not only in the first person but in the present tense in Katniss's voice. It was almost as if the character was insisting on telling this story herself. I never made a concentrated effort to get inside her head, she was already alive in mine."[49] The voice that Collins heard seemed fully formed, complete with a faint Appalachian accent because Collins imagined Katniss as dwelling in Appalachia, the area in the eastern United States that follows the spine of the Appalachian Mountains from New York State to Mississippi. Julie Just, children's book editor of the *New York Times*, calls the character and voice of Katniss "one of the huge strengths" of the book, adding, "she's an utterly tough and memorable heroine."[50]

Political Overtones

By telling the story from the perspective of Katniss, the reader is allowed to witness an individual's political awakening. As she travels to the lavish Capitol and prepares to take part in the games, Katniss is increasingly aware of the deep injustice not only of the games but also of the excesses of the ruling class.

While Katniss struggles with the unfairness of her world, Collins hopes her readers will think of their own time. As she explains to *Scholastic Instructor*, "Telling a story in a futuristic world gives you this freedom to explore things that bother you in contemporary times. So, in the case of *The Hunger Games*, issues like the vast discrepancy of wealth, the power of television and how it's used to influence our lives, the possibility that the government could use hunger as a weapon, and then first and foremost to me, the issue of war."[51]

The Reality Television Effect

The ethical questions surrounding violence have been on Collins's mind since she was a little girl following her father around a battlefield. These questions were a significant part of the *Gregor* series and are also at the core of *The Hunger Games*. But another issue is of major concern in *The Hunger Games*: the effects of reality television.

Collins spent eighteen years as a television writer, and over that time she witnessed the rise of reality television. In *The Hunger Games* series, she grapples with the significance of this genre's domination of the airwaves. She considers what it means for privacy and questions how reality television mimics the way tyrannical governments use surveillance. She also reflects on what reality television does to the viewer's understanding of what is real and what is faked.

Unlike the carefully constructed fictional worlds that Collins created as a television writer, today's reality television urges viewers to

Collins used the idea of enjoyment found in watching others' struggles, such as for competitive reality television shows like **Project Runway** *and* **The Biggest Loser,** *to prompt Katniss's journey in* **The Hunger Games.**

watch supposedly "real" people going through "real" emotional turmoil. Collins seems concerned with the voyeurism this encourages, and reviewers have noted this. The *New York Times*'s Just, for example, describes *The Hunger Games* as "evok[ing] both *Project Runway* and *The Biggest Loser*, but with weapons. There's a voyeurism in the culture that [Collins has] captured."[52]

In addition to voyeurism, Collins tackles the issue of how American television reduces important moments—even real deaths in real wars—into trivial moments. In her opinion, reality television "desensitiz[es] the audience so that when they see real tragedy playing out on the news, it doesn't have the impact it should," she tells *Scholastic Instructor*. "I think it's very important not just for young people, but for adults to make sure they're making the distinction. Because [to] the young soldiers dying in the war in Iraq, it's not going to end at the commercial break … it's not a game. It's your life."[53]

Packaging Violence

The manuscript Collins turned in to editor Kate Egan at Scholastic was dark and political, but in a different way than the *Gregor* series. While characters fought and died in the Underland Chronicles, there is nothing like the graphic descriptions of kid-on-kid violence that appear in *The Hunger Games*.

In one scene, for example, Katniss shoots another tribute. Collins writes, "My arrow drives deeply into the center of his neck. He falls to his knees and halves the brief remainder of his life by yanking out the arrow and drowning in his own blood."[54] Given the level of violence, Scholastic decided to recommend these books for an older audience than that of the *Gregor* series. *The Hunger Games* is meant for readers aged twelve and up. David Levithan, executive editorial director at Scholastic, explains. "If we tried to do the same story at a middle-grade level, it would have been difficult. It was freeing, knowing it was for older readers."[55] Once the editors at Scholastic decided to target a slightly older audience, Collins was free to explore darker topics and discover if such a violent and political book would resonate with readers.

Dystopias

The Hunger Games' Panem is an example of a dystopia. A dystopia is a society that controls and oppresses its population while claiming to be a utopia, or ideal community. One of Collins's favorite books as a young adult, *Nineteen Eighty-Four* by George Orwell, takes place in a dystopia where the population lives under constant surveillance.

In recent years, some critics have noticed a rise in dystopian literature for young adults. Novels in this trend include Margaret Peterson Haddix's Shadow Children series about a society gripped by famine; Scott Westerfeld's The Uglies series, set in a dystopia where everyone is forced to undergo plastic surgery at age sixteen; and James Dashner's Maze Runner trilogy about boys who are trapped in an enclosed environment and forced to survive on their own. Collins speculates that dystopian literature helps young people cope with today's uncertainties. "I think right now there's a distinct uneasiness in the country that the kids feel," she says, citing the economy and the wars in Iraq and Afghanistan. "Dystopian stories are places where you can play out the scenarios in your head—your anxieties—and see what might come of them."

Quoted in Hillel Italie. "How Has 'Hunger Games' Author Suzanne Collins' Life Changed?," *Huffington Post*, September 23, 2010. www.huffingtonpost.com/2010/09/23/hunger-games-suzanne-collins_n_736441.html.

The Hunger Games Hits the Stands

The Hunger Games was published in the fall of 2008. It hit the stands around the same time as *The Twilight Saga: Breaking Dawn*, by Stephenie Meyer, and *Brisingr* by Christopher Paolini, two young-adult books by authors who already had a huge following. Both Meyer's and Paoli's publishers anticipated big sales for these books; the initial print run was 3.2 million copies of *Breaking Dawn* and 2.5 million of *Brisingr.* Scholastic started with a

The Hunger Games *hit book shelves in 2008, around the same time as the fourth book in the hugely popular Twilight series*, Breaking Dawn. *Despite the stiff competition, Collins's book got great reviews and was named best book of the year.*

modest printing of 200,000 copies of *The Hunger Games*, expecting Collins would be overshadowed by Meyer and Paolini.

Yet Collins's book garnered early buzz from reviewers and book buyers who received advance copies of the books. "It's as accessible as Harry Potter," declared Carol Chittenden, owner of Eight Cousins Children's Books in Falmouth, Massachusetts, and children's book buyer for BookStream. "It's going to be a major book."[56] *Publishers Weekly*, a trade journal that covers the book business, predicted, "Though much attention this fall will be lavished on two hotly anticipated YA [young-adult] titles, Stephenie Meyer's *Breaking Dawn* and Christopher Paolini's *Brisingr*, there's always room for a breakout... . From all indications, a prime candidate is Suzanne Collins's *The Hunger Games*."[57]

Publisher Weekly and Chittenden's predictions turned out to be spot on. *The Hunger Games* spent more than one hundred consecutive weeks on the *New York Times* best-seller list. Critics lauded the book's fast-paced, suspenseful plot and careful rendering of a realistic dystopia. John Green in the *New York Times* called the book "brilliantly plotted and perfectly paced."[58] It was named "best book of the year" by *Booklist* and *Publishers Weekly*.

Crossing Over

While the accolades kept rolling in, booksellers noticed something about *The Hunger Games* that distinguished it from the Underland Chronicles. Adults seemed to be buying the book as much as young adults were. Scholastic's decision to categorize the book for an older audience did more than free up Collins to follow the dark and violent plotlines she had conceived. It also meant the book appealed to a broader spectrum of readers.

Like the Harry Potter and the Twilight series, *The Hunger Games* had cross-generational appeal that stood to make it a worldwide phenomenon. As Lizzie Shurnick of *Time* magazine writes, "[Collins is] a literary fusioneer, that rare writer who is all things to all readers."[59] Collins, however, did not stop to think about the runaway success of *The Hunger Games*. She was too busy writing the second and third books in the series.

Writing in a Frenzy

The Hunger Games ends with a cliff-hanger that demands a sequel. Collins immediately set about writing the second book without stopping to consider what the success of the first book might mean. As quickly as she had written the *Gregor* series, she wrote the *Hunger Games* trilogy even faster: She overlapped revising and editing one book with starting the next. In order to keep to her strict publishing schedule, Collins carefully plans her books before writing them, but also leaves herself space to explore new ideas. She explains, "It helps me to work out the key structural points before I begin a story.... I leave some uncharted room for the characters to develop. And if a door opens along the way and I'm intrigued by where it leads I will definitely go through it."[60]

As she wrote, Collins focused on the things that mattered most to her as a writer: exploring contemporary social themes, creating compelling action, and asking her young readers to think about complex ethical issues. Although this series is known for its graphic depiction of violence, Collins does not relish writing about death. She says the scenes in which her characters die are the hardest to write. As she tells Margolis, "When you're going to write a story like *The Hunger Games*, you have to accept from the beginning that you're going to kill characters. It's a horrible

While writing **The Hunger Games,** *Collins took breaks from the book to write more lighthearted fare for the preschoolers' animated series* **Wow! Wow! Wubbzy!**

thing to do, and it's a horrible thing to write, particularly when you have to take out a character that is vulnerable or young or someone you've grown to love when you were writing them."[61]

One of the things that helped her through those difficult passages was taking breaks to work on *Wow! Wow! Wubbzy!*, a lighthearted animated series for children aged two to five that aired on Nick Jr. "When I was working on *The Hunger Games*—there's not a lot of levity in it—I'd do a *Wubbzy* script," she tells *Scholastic Instructor*. "It's an enormous relief to spend some hours in Wuzzleburg … where I know things are going to work out just fine and all the characters will be alive at the end of the program."[62] There were no such assurances in *The Hunger Games*, but Collins felt the violent scenes were necessary because of the issues she felt compelled to explore. These issues—hunger, violence, voyeurism, inequality—drove the action of the *Hunger Games* trilogy. Readers wanted to explore these issues as well, and with each book the trilogy became increasingly popular.

"War. For Adolescents."

As the popularity of The Hunger Games trilogy grew, Collins joined the ranks of J.K. Rowling and Stephenie Meyer, two young-adult authors who sell millions of books, appeal to both children and adults, and have franchises that include films, video games, and other merchandise. Like Rowling and Meyer, Collins developed a loyal fan base and was courted by movie studios for

Suzanne Collins prefers to keep busy writing her books rather than promoting them with appearances and interviews. Book sales have not suffered for her lack of attention. They made several best-seller lists and book stores sold out quickly.

the rights to turn her books into films. This media-shy writer, however, does not relish her position as a "celebrity" author. It is more important to her that her books inspire a love for reading than that they net her fame and wealth. She focuses on using the popularity of her books to encourage young people to think about the day's most pressing social and political issues.

Focus on Writing

In 2009, Scholastic released the second installment in The Hunger Games series, *Catching Fire*. This sequel picks up after Katniss wins the Hunger Games along with Peeta Mellark, another tribute from District 12, and in order to get them both out of the deadly games, Katniss manipulates the Gamemakers and in the process accidentally sparks a rebellion against the Capitol. In *Catching Fire,* the Gamemakers get their revenge; Peeta and Katniss are forced to return to the arena for the seventy-fifth anniversary of the Hunger Games, for an all-star version of the game. Only this time, some of the tributes stop playing each other and start playing against the game. Katniss and another tribute escape, and Katniss discovers the existence of a thirteenth district, in which rebels are planning to overthrow the government. Katniss is also reunited with Gale, her friend, hunting partner, and potential love interest from District 12.

Because the first book was so popular, movie studios started jockeying for the rights to adapt it into a movie while Collins was still writing the sequel. Meanwhile Scholastic was planning a big marketing push for *Catching Fire*. But neither distracted Collins while she was writing the book. Even after she made a deal with Lionsgate for the film rights, she stuck to her rigorous writing schedule and largely avoided interviews about the film.

Collins worked closely with the people who helped her realize the Underland Chronicles and made her first volume of the Hunger Games series a success. She kept Rosemary Stimola as her agent, whom she considers a friend as well as a "gifted creative advisor and professional guardian."[63] She also worked with the same team of editors at Scholastic and remained good friends with James Proimos, the man who suggested she try writing books in the first place. Proimos was not the only writer from her television days that Collins maintained a friendship with. She also stayed close with Peter Bakalian, her collaborator on *Santa Baby!*

The Hunger Games **Phenomenon**

Anticipation was high for *Catching Fire*. Readers could not wait to find out what would happen to Katniss after she returned to District 12 a victor, but one who had defied the Capitol. Scholastic released a limited number of advance copies to librarians and reviewers to pique interest in the second installment. Cindy Dobrez, a middle-school librarian in Holland, Michigan, said that dozens of students signed up for the waiting list to read her advance copy before it even arrived in the mail. One student biked over to Dobrez's house at 8:30 A.M. in her pajamas to snag the copy when it was her turn. That young reader read straight through until 2:30 P.M., stopping only to eat a banana.

These advance copies also created early buzz among reviewers, bloggers, and Tweeters. Scholastic decided on an initial print run of 350,000—150,000 more copies than the first run of *The Hunger Games*. The printing quickly sold out as the book landed on the best-seller lists of the *New York Times*, *USA Today*, the *Wall Street Journal*, and *Publishers Weekly*. The fact that the book sold so well is all the more remarkable considering Collins did almost no promotion. She was too busy writing the final book in the series to do a book tour or give many interviews.

"I'm wonderfully shocked and deeply grateful that the book has connected with so many readers,"[64] Collins told *USA Today*. One thing Collins likes about being a popular author is hearing about people who do not normally read picking up her books. As she tells *Scholastic Instructor*, "One of the most memorable things I hear is when someone tells me that my books got a reluctant reader to read."[65] She loves being able to inspire the same kind of enthusiasm for reading in others that she herself had as a child.

Katniss Everdeen: Feminist Heroine?

Critics delighted in comparing Katniss Everdeen, the protagonist in *The Hunger Games*, to Bella Swan, *Twilight*'s main character. Many critics saw a contrast between Bella's passivity and Katniss's feistiness; they argued that Katniss is a feminist answer to Bella. Writing for the *Atlantic*, Meghan Lewit compared "tough-as-nails" Katniss with "swoony Bella" and hoped that the popularity of *The Hunger Games* meant the return of "girl power."[1] Lewit's colleague at the *Atlantic* Noah Berlatsky countered, "At the end of *Twilight*, Bella actually does get power.... . Katniss, conversely, finds that what she desired all along was domestic bliss with her nice-guy suitor and a bunch of kids running around the cottage."[2]

Collins herself has been tight-lipped about whether or not she considers *The Hunger Games* a feminist book, and Katniss is a complex character who resists being easily categorized. Yet bloggers, fans, and critics cannot help themselves from speculating who would win if Katniss and Bella got in a fight.

1. Meghan Lewit. "Casting *The Hunger Games*: In Praise of Katniss Everdeen." *Atlantic*, March 9, 2011. www.theatlantic.com/entertainment/archive/2011/03/casting-the-hunger-games-in-praise-of-katniss-everdeen/72164/.

2. Noah Berlatsky. "'Twilight' vs. 'The Hunger Games': Why Do So Many Grown-Ups Hate Bella?," *Atlantic*, November 15, 2011. www.theatlantic.com/entertainment/archive/2011/11/twilight-vs-hunger-games-why-do-so-many-grown-ups-hate-bella/248439/.

Cliff-Hangers

In addition to connecting with readers, *Catching Fire* also resonated with critics, who were impressed that Collins was able to maintain the energy of the first book. Reviewing the book for the *New York Times*, young-adult author Gabrielle Zevin wrote, "Collins has done that rare thing. She has written a sequel that improves upon the first book."[66] *People* magazine declared

Among the many accolades for Catching Fire, *the sequel to* The Hunger Games, *was being named "Best Read" by teens in the Teen Read Awards.*

Catching Fire the eighth-best book of the year in its list of the ten best books of 2009. The book also made *Time* magazine's top ten fiction books of 2009 and was a *Booklist* Editor's Choice.

In a review for the *Cleveland Plain Dealer,* Rollie Welch wrote, "The very last sentence of *Catching Fire* will leave readers gasping. Not to mention primed for part three."[67] Indeed, fans of The Hunger Games series were buzzing about the bombshell that Collins dropped at the end of *Catching Fire*: Katniss escapes the game and in retribution the Capitol bombs her home district to ashes. Meanwhile Peeta's fate remains unknown.

In 2010, bookstore owners braced for the release of the third and final book in the series, *Mockingjay*. They knew fans would rush the stores for copies the second it became available. This time, Scholastic "embargoed" the book, meaning they did not send out advance copies to reviewers or book buyers. In addition, those who knew about the book—including Collins—were forbidden to talk to the press about it. The embargo created even greater anticipation among readers. "It will be the biggest book in the [young-adult] section, probably for the entire year,"[68] Sarah Hutton, the children's book buyer and store manager at Village Books in Bellingham, Washington, told the *New York Times*.

Midnight Release

The book was released at 12:01 A.M. on August 24 with an initial print run of 1.2 million copies. Collins decided to give a reading and sign books at the Books of Wonder release party. Books of Wonder is an independent bookstore in Manhattan that supported her career from the beginning. About eight years earlier, Books of Wonder was where she gave her first public reading—to a crowd of about a hundred people. This time five hundred fans started lining up outside around 3 P.M. They waited for hours in a drizzling rain to catch a glimpse of the reclusive author.

Some fans were decked out in wings to look like Rue, the eleven-year-old tribute Katniss forms an alliance with in the first book. Others sported T-shirts that said "Team Peeta" or "Team Gale," to indicate which boy the wearer thinks Katniss should end up dating. One fan wore a "Team Katniss" T-shirt to say she thought Katniss ought to remain single. One reader carried a flask to identify with Haymitch, Katniss and Peeta's drunken mentor. But most fans were dressed as Katniss, carrying bows or wearing their versions of the elaborate gowns Katniss was forced to don for her pregame interviews.

One fan, sixteen-year-old Jessica Miln of New Milford, New Jersey, started hand-stitching her costume in June, even before she knew there was going to be a release party. It was based on the wedding dress Katniss wears for an interview in *Catching Fire* that

Collins displays a mockingjay pendant. The mockingjay image appears on all three covers of the Hunger Games series.

transforms from a white gown into a grey mockingjay outfit. (The mockingjay is a bird that serves as a symbol of the rebels.) Another fan, thirteen-year-old Nathan Chazan, came to Books of Wonder all the way from Toronto. High school senior Kelsey Dixon convinced her mother to bring her from Birch Run, Michigan. "She begged and she begged and I caved in,"[69] her mother said.

Just as many adults showed up for the *Mockingjay* release, demonstrating the series' cross-generational appeal. Suzie Townsend, twenty-nine, left work early to be first in line. She planned to stay up all night reading. Her boss even told her she could come into work late the next day. "Last year at Book Expo [in New York City] they were giving out advanced reader copies of *Catching Fire*," said Townsend. "I was living in Philadelphia at the time, and I got up at 6:15 in the morning, got on the train, ran to the Javits Center, [and] got in line for tickets."[70]

A Family Affair

At Books of Wonder, Collins read from the first chapter: "Peeta was taken prisoner. He is thought to be dead. Most likely he is dead."[71] A shocked murmur spread through the crowd. It was the first time they had had any news of this character's fate since the final

The Harry Potter and Twilight Effects

When *Mockingjay* outsold *Eclipse* (the third book in the Twilight series), Collins was thrown unwillingly into a game of young-adult novelist leap-frog. Industry insiders speculated on whether the Hunger Games series as a whole could outsell the Twilight series. The year before, Meyer had found herself in a similar position, when her Twilight books looked like they might outsell J.K. Rowling's Harry Potter series. Meyer had spent twelve months on the *USA Today*'s best-seller list in 2009, breaking Rowling's record.

However, she did not unseat Harry Potter as the best-selling book series in the world. As of April 2011, 450 million copies of the Harry Potter books had been sold. Meyer's series has sold 117 million, and as of April 2012, the Hunger Games trilogy had sold 36.5 million copies of the three books. When *The Hunger Games* movie was released in March 2012, the popularity of the books was expected to increase, and Collins was poised to join this triumvirate of wildly popular young-adult novelists.

The reigning best-selling book series for young adults is J.K. Rowling's Harry Potter series. Collins's Hunger Games series continues to grow in popularity, but no new series has yet unseated Rowling's Harry Potter in sales.

pages of *Catching Fire*. They were also surprised to hear Collins read in a faint Appalachian accent to approximate the voice she had heard as she first started writing *The Hunger Games*.

Though she was pleased by the enthusiasm of her young readers, Collins urged her fans to go to school the next day. She did not want them skipping class to read her book. She also could not resist the temptation to remind them that she sees just as much inequality in this world as there is in Panem. "At the risk of sounding ungrateful, please go to school," she told the crowd. "So many kids in the world never get a chance to. That being said, if you wanted to stay up late reading, I wouldn't be the one taking the flashlight away from you."[72]

Her own children, who were sixteen and ten at the time, came with her to the reading along with her husband, and were sure to be in school the next day. To Collins, her family is a crucial support system that helps her through her long hours toiling alone on her work. She dedicated the final installment of the trilogy to "Cap, Charlie, and Isabel" and in the back thanks her children "for their daily love, their patience, and the joy they bring me." Her husband is also intimately involved in her writing. He read the earliest draft of *The Hunger Games* and has been her "sounding board through the entire series."[73]

Overtaking Twilight

The five hundred fans who crammed into Books of Wonder that rainy August night were only a sliver of her readers. Within a week of its publication, *Mockingjay* had sold 450,000 copies. The third book of the Twilight series, in contrast, had sold 250,000 copies in its first week. "Bella who? These days it's all about Katniss Everdeen,"[74] writes Tina Jordan in *Entertainment Weekly*, referencing the main character of Meyer's books. Critics and commentators had been comparing Collins and Meyer since *The Hunger Games* was released; however the two are not rivals. In fact, Meyer wrote a glowing comment for *The Hunger Games* that appears on the book's jacket: "I was so obsessed with this book," she wrote, "I had to take it with me out to dinner and hide it

Collins signs copies of the third and final book in the Hunger Games series, Mockingjay, which was published in August 2010.

under the edge of the table so I wouldn't have to stop reading.... . *The Hunger Games* is amazing."[75]

Like Meyer, Collins suddenly became a household name. As Hillel Italie notes in the *Huffington Post,* "With the release of *Mockingjay,* an instant chart-topper, Suzanne Collins is a celebrity. Perhaps not the kind you'd spot on the street, but one whose name is known and welcome to millions of readers, young adult and adult."[76]

Becoming a celebrity was not something Collins was prepared for, however. For example, she kept her home phone number, which was listed in the phone book. She had to change her number after she started getting calls from strangers. "Suddenly, there was this shift," she remembers. "Nothing threatening happened or anything, but it is your home and you want it to be private. So I think that was the point where I felt, 'Oh, something different is happening now.'"[77]

Plagiarism?

With greater fame came greater scrutiny. By and large the books have received favorable reviews, but some critics have grumbled that the action gets bogged down in needless details about clothes, weapons, or scenery. Others complained that the love story made the plot drag. "After 150 pages of romantic dithering, I was tapping my foot to move on,"[78] Welch complained of *Catching Fire*.

But a far more serious criticism was that Collins stole the idea for her book. In his review of *The Hunger Games*, author Stephen King noticed a similarity between Collins's work and that of other authors. He wrote: "Readers of *Battle Royale* (by Koushun Takami), *The Running Man*, or *The Long Walk* (those latter two by some guy named [Richard] Bachman) will quickly realize they have visited these TV badlands before."[79] Richard Bachman is a pseudonym (fake name) that King has used for some of his works and is saying that Collins's ideas are not new.

While King was merely noting a similarity, sci-fi bloggers accused Collins of outright plagiarizing *Battle Royale*. This 1999 Japanese novel features a dystopian future where teenagers fight to the death under the orders of a totalitarian state. It was adapted into a controversial film in 2000. "I suppose I should give Ms. Collins props for ~~ripping off~~ exploiting ~~Asian cinema~~ the YA SF [young-adult science fiction] post-apocalyptic niche,"[80] a poster sarcastically noted on the sci-fi blog *The Galaxy Express* (struck text appears in original). There is even a Facebook page called "Hunger Games is a Rip-off of Battle Royale." When Collins heard about the accusations, she was immediately concerned and called Stimola to ask her if she should read *Battle Royale*. Her agent quickly allayed her fears and told her to forget about the other book and concentrate on her own writing.

Staying with Social Issues

Some critics have dismissed the Hunger Games series as just another book about teen drama and call the games an extended metaphor for the high school social scene. They say the fighting in the games is no different from the jockeying that happens in the school lunch line. Laura Miller, a book critic with the *New Yorker*, suggests that *The Hunger Games* be read as "a fever-dream allegory of the adolescent social experience."[81] Collins bristles at this comparison. "I don't write about adolescence," she said. "I write about war. For adolescents."[82]

For Collins, that distinction is at the heart of why she writes what she does. She does not write about violent games to help teens navigate the social minefield of high school. Instead, she believes that if young people are exposed to the concepts surrounding war, then together, as a society, they can make better decisions about when to engage in conflict. "The concept of war, the specifics of war, the nature of war, the ethical ambiguities of war are introduced too late to children," Collins tells Rick Margolis in *School Library Journal*. "If the whole concept of war were introduced to kids at an earlier age, we would have better dialogues going on about it, and we would have a fuller understanding."[83]

"You Can Hope"

The understanding of war that readers are left with at the end of *Mockingjay* is bleak and terrible. Both the rebels and the Capitol forces are willing to slaughter innocent civilians, even children, if it will give them a tactical advantage. Even the war's "heroes" are crippled with a sense of guilt and plagued by images of violence. According to Sue Corbett of *People*, the final book is "the grimmest yet ... a riveting meditation on the costs of war."[84] As Katniss witnesses the destruction around her she comes to a conclusion similar to Gregor's at the end of the Underland Chronicles: that the world would be a better place without violence.

Collins herself is hopeful for a day without war, though she concedes that day is a long way off. She tells Margolis that she hopes the dialogues inspired by her books can lead to a peaceful future. "At one time, the eradication of slave markets in the United States seemed very far off," she points out. "We can evolve as a species. It's not simple, and it's a very long and drawn-out process, but you can hope."[85]

The Hunger Games on the Big Screen

When movie studios started vying for the rights to *The Hunger Games*, Collins was reluctant to make a deal. She was concerned that the violence in her books could be exploited to boost film sales. She found a partner in Lionsgate Entertainment, however, which purchased the film distribution rights to *The Hunger Games* in 2009. Lionsgate wanted to work closely with the author, giving Collins an opportunity to return to her roots as a dramatic writer and leave the isolated world of novelist to come back to collaborative writing. She teamed up with producer Nina Jacobson and director Gary Ross to make sure her vision remained intact as the books made their way to the screen.

Back to Screenwriting

When Lionsgate secured the distribution rights to *The Hunger Games*, Collins was still in the process of finishing *Mockingjay*. Because of the embargo, she was forbidden to tell anyone—even the people working on the film—what happened in the final book. This presented a challenge to the scriptwriters of *The Hunger Games*. In any film adaptation of a book, parts may be cut or altered, but they had to make sure they did not get rid of anything that would make the events in *Mockingjay* impossible. It was like they were writing a story with a secret ending.

The Films of Gary Ross

Gary Ross penned his own version of *The Hunger Games* script before meeting up with Collins. The author was impressed by his sensitivity to the emotional arc but not really surprised. After all, screenwriting runs in Gary Ross's family; his father, Arthur Ross, penned more than thirty movies. Gary Ross's first major success was in 1988 when his screenplay for the Tom Hanks film *Big* netted him an Oscar nomination. His directorial debut was *Pleasantville*, a 1998 film that tells the story of two teenagers caught in the world of a black-and-white sitcom. Ross was also no stranger to book adaptation, having adapted Laura Hillenbrand's *Seabiscuit* into a multi-Oscar-nominated film in 2003.

However, he still had to vie for *The Hunger Games* job. He traveled to London to meet with producer Jacobson, who was on the set of another film she was producing. Jacobson had a long line of interested directors clamoring for the job, but she was looking for someone who would not get caught up in the action and violence of the story and forget the emotional heart of the books. She chose Ross in part because, he has "a real feel for the balancing act between the epic adventure and the intimate love story," she told *Entertainment Weekly*.

Quoted in Karen Valby. "*Hunger Games* Exclusive: Why Gary Ross Got the Coveted Job and Who Suggested Megan Fox for the Lead Role." *Entertainment Weekly*, January 6, 2011. http://insidemovies.ew.com/2011/01/06/hunger-games-exclusive-gary-ross/.

The only solution was for Collins to write the first screenplay herself. Collins told *Entertainment Weekly*, "I knew that if the screenplay got off on the wrong foot, that you could end up with something by which you could never reach the events of the third book. ... I wanted to be around to keep an eye on that."[86] As *Mockingjay* was going through final revisions, Collins started adapting *The Hunger Games* for the big screen.

She drew on her years of experience writing for children's television to sculpt a script that would allow for the sequels. Collins did not have to fight hard to have her voice heard. The team at Lionsgate—including Jacobson and Ross—were big fans of Collins's work and were eager to get her insight. "[Lionsgate] established a dialogue with me," Collins added. "[They made] me feel my input was valuable and welcome."[87]

Fast Friends

Collins was pleased with Jacobson's choice of director; she was a fan of Ross's films *Seabiscuit* and *Pleasantville*. Ross, who got hooked on the trilogy when his kids were reading it, was looking forward to talking with Collins about the script. The two expected they would work well together, but were surprised by how much they agreed. When they met, they had instant creative chemistry and realized they shared a vision for the film. Ross was sensitive to the emotional content of the books. It helped Collins feel confident the movies would be well crafted and nuanced, not just action flicks. When she had an opportunity to sit down with Ross and talk with him about the film, she was so impressed with his understanding of her book that she was "fully on board"[88] with the adaptation.

Ross remembers their first meeting in Los Angeles: "I think we had maybe 15 minutes of discussion, and then we instantly transitioned into writing together seamlessly." He calls her "a real

Director Gary Ross worked closely with Collins to bring her vision to the big screen in **The Hunger Games** *movie.*

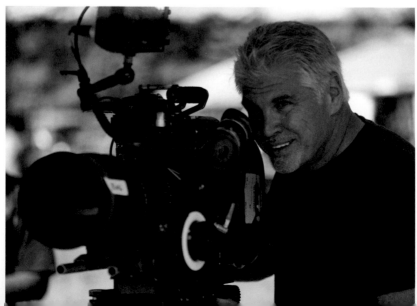

writing partner" and added: "I've found that wonderful collaborative electricity."[89] They came together as a team to merge their ideas into one script. They worked in marathon sessions that went on long past midnight as the two pitched lines back and forth to each other to create the dialogue.

Even after the script was drafted, Ross was impressed by Collins's knowledge of production. He wanted her input on every aspect of the film, from casting to costumes. As the sets were being built, Ross flew Collins out to Los Angeles to get her feedback—and she had valuable notes. For example, she suggested he make the government buildings larger to demonstrate the power and opulence of the Capitol. It was a suggestion he took to heart, and had the set changed accordingly. She also collaborated on costume design and casting. Her busy role kept her "bouncing back and forth between set and home for most of the production."[90] Ross deeply admires the author and hopes that his film will be true to the book and "live up to what Suzanne has done."[91]

Moral Inquiry

For Collins, one of the more challenging aspects of adapting her books into movies is thinking about how the medium of film will complicate the books' ethical questions. "The audience for both the gladiator games and our current reality television shows are almost characters in and of themselves.... They can play a role in [the players'] elimination," she said in a *New York Times Book Review* podcast. "This is one of the most exciting aspects for me [in adapting it for the screen]. If you go to the movie you will be part of the audience in the theater, but will you feel like you're part of the Hunger Games audience as well.... How much will you be caught up in the Capitol's game?"[92]

Luckily, the team working on *The Hunger Games* films is aware of the author's desire to have her work address ethical issues. They too want to preserve that aspect of the books. In other words, they want to make a film that is not only entertaining but will also challenge the viewer to think about what they are watching. Jacobson sees no contradiction between the entertainment value and political message of the book. In fact, she sees the two as connected. "The suspense of *The Hunger Games* is heightened by its spirit of moral inquiry," she says. "Suzanne has entrusted Lionsgate and me to bring that moral perspective to the adaptation—a charge we fully intend to honor."[93]

Collins is very careful that the products associated with her series remain true to her ethical vision and that marketing strategies do not capitalize on the books' violence. For example, she made sure that the online video game based on the books was about strategy, and also that it focused on the training week that precedes the game. She says, "I don't want it to be about kids killing kids."[94] Her involvement in the movie and the shared vision of the film team seem to ensure the resulting films are not an exploitative gore-fest.

Casting *The Hunger Games*

Collins also played a role in casting the film—a process that was controversial from the moment the adaptation was announced. As soon as news of the deal with Lionsgate came out, fan boards, blogs, and online communities started buzzing about how the

Josh Hutcherson, known for his work on Journey to the Center of the Earth, *and* Journey 2: The Mysterious Island, *among other roles, was cast in the role of Peeta Mellark.*

Liam Hemsworth, center, plays Gale in **The Hunger Games** *movie.*

film would be cast. Ross and Collins found their creative chemistry and shared vision carried over from the scriptwriting session into the casting call.

They knew they would have to make hard choices; each reader had formed their own idea of what their favorite characters should look and act like. Eighteen-year-old Josh Hutcherson, who played the son of a lesbian couple in the critically acclaimed *The Kids Are Alright*, auditioned for the part of Peeta, and Ross and Collins knew instantly they had found the perfect actor for the role. They did not even discuss Hutcherson's performance; they just turned to each other and high-fived.

Meanwhile Australian actor Liam Hemsworth snagged the role of Gale. Other actors cast include Woody Harrelson as Haymitch Abernathy, Lenny Kravitz as Cinna (Katniss's doting stylist), and Donald Sutherland as Panem's President Snow. Actor Elizabeth Banks, who worked with Ross on *Seabiscuit*, wrote him a letter telling him how much she loved Collins's trilogy and that she wanted to play Effie Trinket, the semiridiculous escort for the tributes from District 12. After auditions, Ross offered her the part.

Jennifer Lawrence's Previous Roles

Looking at a photo spread of Jennifer Lawrence's red carpet appearance at the 2011 Academy Awards, one can see why her looks gave *Hunger Game* fans pause when she was announced as Katniss. She is a classic blonde bombshell with delicate features and bright blue eyes. But Lawrence has proved herself as an actor who can handle tough parts. Both Collins and Ross had admired her past performances.

Originally from Louisville, Kentucky, Lawrence began acting in 2006 with a series of parts on television shows, including *Monk* and *Cold Case*. Two years later, she had netted parts in three independent films: *Garden Party, The Poker House*, and *The Burning Plain*. Critics singled out her acting for praise, and she won an Outstanding Performance Award at the Los Angeles Film Festival for her role in *The Poker House*. But it was her explosive performance in the 2010 film *Winter's Bone* that brought her widespread recognition and an Oscar nomination for Best Performance by an Actress in a Leading Role. In this gritty film set in the Ozarks, she plays a young woman traveling through the underworld of crystal meth dealers to find her father. Lawrence had to learn how to chop wood, skin squirrels, and fist fight in order to play the role. Shortly thereafter she received her first role in a major motion picture, as Raven/Mystique in *X-Men: First Class*.

Finding the Right Katniss

The most difficult—and controversial—casting choice was for the sixteen-year-old heroine. Meghan Lewit of the *Atlantic* called Katniss "the most important female character in recent pop culture history."[95] Every reader developed a deep attachment to her and had a different idea of what she looked like and which actor could play her best. Early predictions for the role included

Oscar nominee Jennifer Lawrence was cast in the lead role of Katniss. Collins was pleased, but early fan response was not positive. Collins assured fans that they would not be disappointed.

fourteen-year-old Chloe Moretz, who played a child assassin in *Kick Ass*, and Hailee Steinfeld, the young star of *True Grit*.

But Collins and Ross were wowed by the audition of twenty-year-old actor Jennifer Lawrence, who received an Oscar nod for her role in *Winter's Bone*. Ross said Lawrence's reading for the part simply "knocked [him] out."[96] Collins personally called Lawrence to congratulate her after she was offered the role. She told Lawrence that when the actor agreed to take the part, "the world got lifted off my shoulders."[97]

Fans were not as impressed by the casting choice. After Lionsgate announced Lawrence would play the lead in March 2011, a collective groan went up on the Internet. Many fans were dismayed, thinking the twenty-year-old actor was too old to play the part. The even bigger complaint was Lawrence's looks. In the book Katniss is described as having an olive complexion and dark hair, while Lawrence is blonde and pale. Many readers imagined Katniss as biracial and thought the casting "whitewashed" the film. The feminist website Jezebel.com called the decision to cast Lawrence a "missed opportunity"[98] for diversity in Hollywood.

The complaints were so pronounced, Collins felt the need to respond. She wrote an open letter to fans defending the decision in *Entertainment Weekly*: "Could [Lawrence] believably inspire a rebellion? Did she project the strength, defiance, and intellect you would need to follow her into certain war? For me, she did."[99] Ross also weighed in on *Screen Rant*, saying that Lawrence's audition was spectacular. He also assured viewers Lawrence's hair would be dyed to match the color in the book.

Keeping a Low Profile

Filming began in May 2011 in Burke County, North Carolina, and the official trailer was released in November of that year. But even before the film buzz, Collins was a best-selling author. At the time of the 2009 deal with Lionsgate, there were already more than 6 million copies of *The Hunger Games* in print and, by June 2011, Collins became only the sixth writer—and the first young-adult author—to sell more than a million books for the Kindle reading device.

But Collins does not get hung up on sales numbers or fame because she thinks her popularity will inevitably fade. As she tells Susan Dominus of the *New York Times*, "I've been a writer a long time, and right now *The Hunger Games* is getting a lot of focus. It'll pass. The focus will be on something else. It'll shift. It always does. And that seems just fine."[100] Collins maintains a low-tech website, and she does not blog or Tweet. In fact, it is very difficult for fans to access their beloved author. She rarely does interviews and often requests that television cameras be barred from her public appearances.

When asked by the website Goodreads what her skill would be if she had to participate in the Hunger Games, she replied "hiding," and even though she is trained in sword fighting, she added that if she was thrown into the games she would avoid encounters with other players and instead would be "scaling those trees like Katniss and Rue."[101] Collins enjoys her quiet days working at home, where she is kept company by her two cats, Zora and Zable. She calls her cats "very important" and says her family "either rescued or abducted them"[102] when they were feral kittens living in her backyard in Connecticut.

The highly anticipated Hunger Games *movie was released in March 2012.*

Letting Go

Nor is Collins interested in the wealth her popularity brings. In fact, she says her royalties are paid to her a little at a time, so she does not really feel the financial effects of her book sales. Not that it matters to her, because she says she "is not a fancy person."[103] When asked what she would do with a million dollars, she says she would give most to charity and put the rest in savings. She says that mostly she just wants a break. "I'd really like to go on a vacation,"[104] she quips.

With huge sales and a hotly anticipated movie in the works, Collins could cling to *The Hunger Games* for the rest of her career—working on the film sequels or creating additional products like guides or encyclopedias. But Collins is ready to move on to other projects. In November 2011, Lionsgate began negotiation with Simon Beaufoy, the screenwriter who penned *Slumdog Millionaire* and *127 Hours*, to take over scriptwriting responsibilities for *Catching Fire*. "You have to let things go,"[105] Collins told *Entertainment Weekly*.

Moving On

Collins has already moved on from *The Hunger Games* and is working on another—and highly personal—project. In 2012 she was working on an autobiographical children's book about the year her father spent overseas. The book will feature illustrations based on her own family photos. "I specifically want to do this book ... as a sort of memory piece kind of honoring that year for my family," Collins says. But she is—yet again—also writing a book with a purpose. She says this book is also motivated by a desire to reach out to children who are struggling with having a family member serving in the military. She adds that she wants to do the book because "so many children are experiencing it right now—having deployed parents."[106]

Fans who became addicted to the heart-thudding action and who delighted in the strange and violent fictional world of the Hunger Games series may be disappointed in Collins's new book. But Collins is not an author who wants to be defined by one work—even one as popular as *The Hunger Games*.

Introduction: The Thinking Kid's Best Seller

1. Quoted in Hillel Italie. "How Has 'Hunger Games' Author Suzanne Collins' Life Changed?," *Huffington Post,* September 23, 2010. www.huffingtonpost.com/2010/09/23/hunger-games-suzanne-collins_n_736441.html.
2. Laura Miller "Fresh Hell." *New Yorker,* June 14, 2010. www.newyorker.com/arts/critics/atlarge/2010/06/14/100614crat_atlarge_miller#ixzz1fgOwn1SS.
3. Lev Grossman. "*Catching Fire:* Suzanne Collins' Hit Young-Adult Novels." *Time,* September 7, 2009. www.time.com/time/magazine/article/0,9171,1919156,00.html#ixzz1gS7OobqV.

Chapter 1: An Unsheltered Childhood

4. Quoted in Susan Dominus. "Suzanne Collins's War Stories for Kids." *New York Times Magazine,* April 8, 2011. www.nytimes.com/2011/04/10/magazine/mag-10collins-t.html?_r=1&pagewanted=all.
5. Quoted in Rick Margolis. "A Killer Story: An Interview with Suzanne Collins, Author of 'The Hunger Games.'" *School Library Journal,* September 1, 2008. www.schoollibraryjournal.com/article/CA6590063.html.
6. Quoted in Scholastic. "A Conversation: Question and Answers, Suzanne Collins, Author of *The Hunger Games* Trilogy." www.scholastic.com/thehungergames/media/suzanne_collins_q_and_a.pdf.
7. Quoted in Dominus. "Suzanne Collins's War Stories for Kids."
8. Quoted in Dominus. "Suzanne Collins's War Stories for Kids."

9. Quoted in Rick Margolis. "The Last Battle: With 'Mockingjay' on Its Way, Suzanne Collins Weighs in on Katniss and the Capitol." *School Library Journal*, August 2010. www.school libraryjournal.com/slj/home/885800-312/the_last_battle_ with_mockingjay.html.csp.

10. Quoted in Scholastic. "A Conversation: Question and Answers, Suzanne Collins, Author of *The Hunger Games Trilogy*."

11. Quoted in Hannah Trierweiler Hudson. "Q & A with *Hunger Games* Author Suzanne Collins: The Author of *The Hunger Games* Says We Need to Get Real About War, Violence, and TV." *Scholastic Instructor*, September–October 2010. www .scholastic.com/teachers/article/qa-hunger-games-author-suzanne-collins.

12. Quoted in Scholastic. "A Conversation: Question and Answers, Suzanne Collins."

13. Quoted in *Scholastic* videos. Author interviews. Suzanne Collins, Interview 2. www.scholastic.com/browse/video .jsp?pID=1640183585&bcpid=1640183585&bclid=1745 181007&bctid=1840656769.

14. Eric Berman. "'Forest Game' Is a Suspenseful, Successful Play." *Indiana Daily Student*, December 4, 1984.

15. Quoted in *Scholastic* videos. Author interviews.

Chapter 2: From the Stage to the Small Screen

16. Quoted in *Scholastic* videos. Author interviews.

17. Quoted in Margolis. "The Last Battle."

18. Classic Stage Company. "Our Mission." http://classicstage .org/mission.shtml.

19. Quoted in Teen Reads. Author Talk.

20. Lisanne Renner. "Nickelodeon's 25th Year: Care for a Slice of Slime?," *New York Times*, June 13, 2004, p. C59.

21. Quoted in *Scholastic* videos. Author interviews.

22. James Sterngold. "Looking for Laughs? Call a Harvard Grad: As Writers and Producers, Young Alumni Find They Can

Make a Lot of Money Fast from Harvard to a Job in TV Comedy Writing." *New York Times*, August 27, 1997. www.nytimes.com/1997/08/26/arts/as-writers-and-producers-young-alumni-find-they-can-make-a-lot-of-money-fast.html?scp=1&sq=sterngold%20looking%20for%20laughs?&st=cse&pagewanted=2.

23. Quoted in T.L. Stanley. "'Shelby' Cracks Saturday Lineup." *Mediaweek,* January 6, 1997, p. 9.
24. Quoted in Italie. "How Has 'Hunger Games' Author Suzanne Collins' Life Changed?"
25. Quoted in *Scholastic* videos. Author interviews.
26. Suzanne Collins.com. "Biography—Suzanne Collins." www.suzannecollinsbooks.com/bio.htm.
27. Quoted in *Scholastic* videos. Author interviews.

Chapter 3: The World Below

28. Quoted in *Scholastic* videos. Author interviews.
29. Quoted in an interview with Jen Rees. Suzanne Collins website. www.suzannecollinsbooks.com/events.htm.
30. Quoted in Margolis, "The Last Battle.
31. Quoted in *Scholastic* video clips for Suzanne Collins's *Hunger Games.* "Similarities to the Underland." www.scholastic.com/thehungergames/videos/similarities-to-underland.htm.
32. Quoted in Italie. "How Has *Hunger Games* Author Suzanne Collins' Life Changed?"
33. Steven Engelfried et al. Review of *Gregor the Overlander. School Library Journal*, September 2003.
34. *Publishers Weekly.* Review of *Gregor the Overlander*, September 8, 2003, p. 77.
35. *Kirkus Review.* Review of *Gregor the Overlander*, September 2003.
36. Quoted in an interview with Jen Rees.
37. Quoted in an interview with Jen Rees.
38. Tasha Saecker. Review of *Gregor and the Curse of the Warmbloods. School Library Journal*, September 2006, p. 100.

39. *Kirkus Reviews*. Review of *Gregor and the Curse of the Warmbloods*. June, 2005.
40. Quoted in Hudson. "Q & A with *Hunger Games Author* Suzanne Collins."
41. Gabrielle Zevin. "Constant Craving." *New York Times Book Review*, October 9, 2009. www.nytimes.com/2009/10/11/books/review/Zevin-t.html.
42. Quoted in Margolis. "The Last Battle."
43. Kitty Flynn. Review of *Gregor and the Code of Claw*: Book Five in the Underland Chronicles. *Horn Book Magazine*, July/August 2007, p. 392.
44. Suzanne Collins. *Gregor and the Code of Claw*. New York: Scholastic Press, 2007, p. 411.

Chapter 4: A Breakout Hit

45. Quoted in Scholastic. "A Conversation: Question and Answers, Suzanne Collins."
46. Quoted in Goodreads. "5 Questions with Suzanne Collins: Author of the *Hunger Games* Trilogy." www.goodreads.com/videos/show/10432-5-questions-with-suzanne-collins-author-of-the-hunger-games-trilogy.
47. Quoted in Scholastic. "A Conversation: Question and Answers, Suzanne Collins."
48. Quoted in Margolis. "A Killer Story."
49. Quoted in *New York Times Book Review* podcast, August 27, 2010. http://graphics8.nytimes.com/podcasts/2010/08/27/27bookreview.mp3.
50. Quoted in *New York Times Book Review* podcast.
51. Quoted in Hudson. "Q & A with *Hunger Games* Author Suzanne Collins."
52. Quoted in *New York Times Book Review* podcast.
53. Quoted in Hudson. "Q & A with *Hunger Games* Author Suzanne Collins."
54. Suzanne Collins. *The Hunger Games*. New York: Scholastic Books, 2008, p. 233.

55. Quoted in John A. Sellers. "A Dark Horse Breaks Out." *Publishers Weekly*, June 9, 2008. www.publishersweekly .com/pw/print/20080609/9915-a-dark-horse-breaks-out .html.

56. Quoted in Sellers. "A Dark Horse Breaks Out."

57. Sellers. "A Dark Horse Breaks Out."

58. John Green. "Scary New World." *New York Times*, November 7, 2008, p. 30.

59. Lizzie Skurnick. "Suzanne Collins." The 2010 *Time* 100: Artists. *Time*, April 29, 2010. www.time.com/time/specials/ packages/article/0,28804,1984685_1984940_1985512,00 .html.

60. Quoted in Goodreads. "5 Questions with Suzanne Collins."

61. Quoted in Margolis. "A Killer Story."

62. Quoted in Hudson. "Q & A with *Hunger Games* Author Suzanne Collins."

Chapter Five: "War. For Adolescents."

63. Suzanne Collins. *Mockingjay*. New York, NY: Scholastic Books, 2010. Acknowledgements.

64. Quoted in Carol Memmott, Bob Minzesheimer, and Deirdre Donahue. "Book Buzz: What's New on the List and in Publishing." *USA Today*, September 10, 2009. www .usatoday.com/life/books/news/2009-09-09-book-buzz_ N.htm.

65. Quoted in Hudson. "Q & A with *Hunger Games* Author Suzanne Collins."

66. Zevin. "Constant Craving."

67. Rollie Welch. "'Catching Fire' Brings Back Suzanne Collins' Kindhearted Killer." *Cleveland Plain Dealer*, September 6, 2009. www.cleveland.com/bookreviews/plaindealer/ index.ssf?/base/entertainment-1/125213948127050 .xml&coll=2.

68. Quoted in Julie Bosman. "Booksellers brace for *Mockingjay* landing." *New York Times*, August, 24 2010. Page C1.

69. Quoted in Hillel Italie. "*Mockingjay* Receives Midnight Launch at NYC Store." *Boston Globe,* August 25, 2010. www.boston.com/ae/books/articles/2010/08/24/mockingjay_receives_midnight_launch_at_nyc_store/.

70. Quoted in Jada Yuan and Alex Reese. "Meet the Obsessed *Mockingjay* Fans Who Turned Up for the Book's Midnight Release." *New York Magazine*, August 25, 2010. http://nymag.com/daily/entertainment/2010/08/mockingjay.html#photo=9x58909.

71. Collins. *Mockingjay*, p. 4.

72. Quoted in Bob Minzesheimer. "Teen Alert: *Mockingjay* Arrives Early Tuesday; and We Mean Early, 12:01 a.m., for Trilogy Finale." *Life*, August 19, 2010, p. 1D.

73. Collins. *Mockingjay*, Acknowledgments.

74. Tina Jordan. "Suzanne Collins on the Books She Loves." *Entertainment Weekly*, August 13, 2010. www.ew.com/ew/article/0,,20419951_20417110,00.html.

75. Quoted at www.suzannecollinsbooks.com.

76. Quoted in Italie. "How Has *Hunger Games* Author Suzanne Collins' Life Changed?"

77. Quoted in Italie. "How Has *Hunger Games* Author Suzanne Collins' Life Changed?"

78. Rollie Welch. "*Catching Fire* Brings Back Suzanne Collins' Kindhearted Killer."

79. Stephen King. Review of *The Hunger Games. Entertainment Weekly,* September 8, 2008. www.ew.com/ew/article/0,,20223443,00.html.

80. Quoted in Heather Massey. "*The Hunger Games* vs. *Battle Royale.*" *The Galaxy Express* (blog), March 30, 2010. www.thegalaxyexpress.net/2010/03/hunger-games-vs-battle-royale.html.

81. Miller. "Fresh Hell."

82. Quoted in Dominus. "I Write About War. For Adolescents."

83. Quoted in Margolis. "The Last Battle."

84. Sue Corbett. "Picks and Pans." *People,* September 13, 2010. www.people.com/people/archive/article/0,,20418879,00.html.

85. Quoted in Margolis. "The Last Battle."

Chapter Six: *The Hunger Games* on the Big Screen

86. Quoted in Karen Valby. "Team 'Hunger Games' Talks: Author Suzanne Collins and Director Gary Ross on Their Allegiance to Each Other, and Their Actors." *Entertainment Weekly*, April 7, 2011. http://insidemovies.ew.com/2011/04/07/hunger-games-suzanne-collins-gary-ross-exclusive/.

87. Quoted in Tina Jordan. "Suzanne Collins on Writing a *Hunger Games* Movie: 'You Have to Let Things Go.'" *Entertainment Weekly*, December 9, 2010. http://shelf-life.ew.com/2010/12/09/hunger-games-suzanne-collins/

88. Quoted in Valby. "Team 'Hunger Games' Talks."

89. Quoted in Valby. "Team 'Hunger Games' Talks."

90. Quoted in Valby. "Team 'Hunger Games' Talks."

91. Quoted in Krista Smith. "*Hunger Games* Director Gary Ross on Jennifer Lawrence's Powerful Acting: 'It's Like Looking into a Blast Furnace.'" *Vanity Fair*, The Hollywood Blog, November 11, 2011. www.vanityfair.com/online/oscars/2011/11/qa-gary-ross-on-hunger-games-jennifer-lawrence.

92. Quoted in *New York Times Book Review* podcast.

93. Lionsgate Investors. "LIONSGATE® Feasts on THE HUNGER GAMES." March 17, 2009. http://investors.lionsgate.com/phoenix.zhtml?c=62796&p=irol-newsArticle&ID=1267040&highlight=.

94. Quoted in *New York Times Book Review* podcast.

95. Meghan Lewit. "Casting *The Hunger Games*: In Praise of Katniss Everdeen." *Atlantic*, March 9, 2011. www.theatlantic.com/entertainment/archive/2011/03/casting-the-hunger-games-in-praise-of-katniss-everdeen/72164/.

96. Quoted in Ben Kindrick. "*Hunger Games* Director Gary Ross Talks Casting Jennifer Lawrence." *Screen Rant*, March 17, 2011. http://screenrant.com/gary-ross-hunger-games-jennifer-lawrence-benk-106673/.

97. Quoted in EW Staff. "This Week's Cover: First Look at Jennifer Lawrence as Katniss in 'The Hunger Games.'" *Entertainment Weekly*, May 8, 2011. http://popwatch.ew.com/2011/05/18/the-hunger-games-jennifer-lawrence-first-look-exclusive/.

98. Jezebel. "The Imminent Whitewashing of *The Hunger Games'* Heroine," March 14, 2011. http://jezebel.com/5781682/the-imminent-whitewashing-of-the-hunger-games-heroine.

99. Quoted in Darren Franich. "*Hunger Games*: Suzanne Collins Talks Jennifer Lawrence as Katniss." Inside Movies. *Entertainment Weekly,* March 21, 2010. http://insidemovies.ew.com/2011/03/21/hunger-games-suzanne-collins-jennifer-lawrence/.

100. Quoted in Dominus. "I Write About War. For Adolescents."

101. Quoted in Goodreads. "5 Questions with Suzanne Collins."

102. Quoted in *Scholastic* video clips for Suzanne Collins's *Hunger Games.* "Getting Personal." www.scholastic.com/thehungergames/videos/getting-personal.htm.

103. Quoted in Dominus. "I Write About War. For Adolescents."

104. Quoted in Goodreads. "5 Questions with Suzanne Collins."

105. Quoted in Jordan. "Suzanne Collins on Writing *The Hunger Games* Movie."

106. Quoted in Dominus. "I Write About War. For Adolescents."

1962

Suzanne Collins is born on August 11 to Michael and Jane Collins in New Jersey, the youngest of three girls and a boy.

1968

Michael Collins serves in Vietnam, and the rest of the family moves to Indiana.

1972

Michael Collins accepts post with NATO and moves the family to Brussels, Belgium.

1974

Suzanne, now twelve, declares she wants to be an actor, a career she pursues until she turns twenty.

1978

The Collins family returns to the United States, where Collins finishes her last two years of high school.

1980

Collins enrolls at Indiana University (IU) in Bloomington. There she meets Cap Pryor, her future husband.

1982

Collins writes her first one-act play and decides to pursue a career as a dramatic writer.

1986

Collins graduates from IU with a bachelor of arts degree in theater and drama and telecommunications.

1987

Collins moves to New York City to attend New York University's Tisch School of the Arts in order to earn a master's degree in dramatic writing.

1991

Collins begins writing for children television, collaborating on scripts for shows on Nickelodeon and Nick Jr.

1993

Receives first scriptwriters credit for an episode of *Clarissa Explains It All* for Nickelodeon; begins writing for *The Mystery Files of Shelby Woo.*

1994

Gives birth to her first child, Charlie.

1995

Writes for *Little Bear* on Nick Jr.

2000

Gives birth to her second child, Isabel; starts working with James Proimos on *Generation O!;* Proimos suggests she try writing a novel.

2001

Cowrites Christmas special *Santa Baby!* with Peter Bakalian.

2002

Leaves New York City for Connecticut; begins writing first novel.

2003

Secures agent, Rosemary Stimola; publishes *Gregor the Overlander* with Scholastic Press.

2004

Publishes *Gregor and the Prophecy of Bane; Gregor the Overlander* wins New Atlantic Independent Booksellers Association book of the year award.

2005

Publishes *When Charlie McButton Lost Power* and *Gregor and the Curse of the Warmbloods*; starts writing for *Clifford's Puppy Days*, an animated series on PBS.

2006

Publishes *Gregor and the Marks of Secret*; signs a six-figure deal for The Hunger Games trilogy.

2007

Publishes *Gregor and the Code of Claw; Gregor and the Marks of Secret* wins Oppenheim Toy Portfolio Gold Award; begins writing *The Hunger Games.*

2008

Publishes *The Hunger Games; The Hunger Games* is a *New York Times* notable book; *Publishers Weekly, School Library Journal, Kirkus Reviews,* and *Booklist* all name *The Hunger Games* the best book of the year; begins writing for television show *Wow! Wow! Wubbzy!*

2009

Publishes *Catching Fire,* which lands on the best-seller lists of the *New York Times, USA Today, Wall Street Journal,* and *Publishers Weekly; Catching Fire* makes the top ten list for *Time* and *People* magazine; Lionsgate purchases distribution rights to *The Hunger Games.*

2010

Publishes *Mockingjay* on August 25; *Mockingjay* sells 450,000 copies in its first week, outselling Stephenie Meyer's *Eclipse;*

Mockingjay makes best-seller lists of the *New York Times, Wall Street Journal,* and *Publisher's Weekly,* among others; *Entertainment Weekly* names Collins entertainer of the year; named one of *Time* 100 (most influential people in the world); preproduction begins for *The Hunger Games* movie.

2011

Becomes the sixth author to join the Kindle Million Club; filming begins for *The Hunger Games* movie; begins writing autobiographical children's book on her father's deployment to Vietnam.

2012

The Hunger Games movie released.

For More Information

Books

Suzanne Collins. *The World of the Hunger Games*. Scholastic, 2012. An illustrated guide to the world of the Hunger Games, including information on the districts, Katniss's life, and biographies of all the participants.

Lois H. Gresh. *The "Hunger Games" Companion: The Unauthorized Guide to the Series*. St. Martin's Press, 2011. Contains background information on the games, analysis of the book's themes, and an unauthorized biography of the author.

Leah Wilson, ed. *The Girl Who Was on Fire: Your Favorite Authors on Suzanne Collins' "Hunger Games" Trilogy*. Dallas: BenBella Books, 2011. A collection of essays from a variety of authors exploring various themes in the trilogy, including fashion, politics, and psychology.

Periodicals

Hillel Italie. "Top 10 'Challenged' Books: Suzanne Collins, Sherman Alexie Novels Draw Criticism." *Seattle Times*, April 11, 2011.

Kevin Maher. "As *Twilight* Fades, Prepare for *The Hunger Games*; with the Vampire Franchise Upping Stakes, the Bleak World of *The Hunger Games* Is Set to Lure Teen Fans to the Multiplexes. Kevin Maher Meets Its Makers." *Times* (London), November 11, 2011.

Rick Margolis. "The Last Battle: With *Mockingjay* on Its Way, Suzanne Collins Weighs in on Katniss and the Capitol." *School Library Journal*, August 2010.

Karen Springen. "Unhappily Ever After; Remember When Children's Books Frolicked Through Tales of Ponies and Princes? The Latest Kid-Lit Craze Is Stories About Living Through the Apocalypse—Now." *Newsweek*, July 21, 2008.

Internet Sources

Jorge Carreon. "Literary Youthquake: A Q&A with Author Suzanne Collins and "The Hunger Games." *Los Angeles Examiner,* January 6, 2009. www.examiner.com/personalities-in-los-angeles/literary-youthquake-a-q-a-with-author-suzanne-collins-and-the-hunger-games.

Susan Dominus. "I Write About War. For Adolescents." *New York Times Magazine*, April 8, 2011. www.nytimes.com/2011/04/10/magazine/mag-10collins-t.html?_r=1&pagewanted=all.

Shannon Firth. "Suzanne Collins, Author of "The Hunger Games" and "The Underland Chronicles." FindingDulcinea, April 9, 2010. www.findingdulcinea.com/features/profiles/c/suzanne-collins.html.

Hannah Trierweiler Hudson. "Q & A with *Hunger Games* Author Suzanne Collins: The Author of *The Hunger Games* Says We Need to Get Real About War, Violence, and TV." *Scholastic Instructor*, September–October 2010. www.scholastic.com/teachers/article/qa-hunger-games-author-suzanne-collins.

Hillel Italie. "How Has 'Hunger Games' Author Suzanne Collins' Life Changed?," *Huffington Post*, September 23, 2010. www.huffingtonpost.com/2010/09/23/hunger-games-suzanne-collins_n_736441.html.

Tina Jordan. "Suzanne Collins on the Books She Loves." EW.com, August 13, 2010. www.ew.com/ew/article/0,,20419951_20417110,00.html.

Laura Miller. "Fresh Hell." *New Yorker*, June 14, 2010. www.newyorker.com/arts/critics/atlarge/2010/06/14/100614crat_atlarge_miller.

Laura Miller. "*The Hunger Games* vs. *Twilight*." *Salon*, September 5, 2010. www.salon.com/2010/09/05/hunger_games_twilight.

Lynn Neary. "Edgy, Violent Thrillers for the Teen-Age Set." *All Things Considered*, September 1, 2009. www.npr.org/templates/story/story.php?storyId=112119277.

Nina Rastogi. "Suzanne Collins, Author of the *Hunger Games* Trilogy." *Slate*, July 26, 2011. www.slate.com/articles/technology/top_right/2011/07/suzanne_collins_author_of_the_hunger_games_trilogy.html.

Karen Valby. "Team 'Hunger Games' Talks: Author Suzanne Collins and Director Gary Ross on Their Allegiance to Each Other, and Their Actors." *Entertainment Weekly*, April 7, 2011. http://insidemovies.ew.com/2011/04/07/hunger-games-suzanne-collins-gary-ross-exclusive.

Natalie Zutter. "Snap This: Suzanne Collins Gets in on the *Hunger Games* Fun." Crushable, July 4, 2011. http://crushable.com/entertainment/snap-this-suzanne-collins-gets-in-on-the-hunger-games-fun.

Websites

Hunger Games (www.scholastic.com/thehungergames). The Scholastic website contains video author interviews, information about the books, and video games.

Mockingjay (http://mockingjay.net/). Originally meant to focus on the books, this popular fan site features podcasts, discussion forums, and news about both the novels and the film.

My Hunger Games (www.myhungergames.com). Updated daily, this site contains news on the film, books, and interviews with actors cast in the films.

Suzanne Collins (www.suzannecollinsbooks.com). The author's website contains an interview, information on each book, and a brief biography.

The Underland Chronicles (www.scholastic.com/underlandchronicles/). Hosted by Scholastic Press, this site contains maps of the Underland, an interview with Collins, and a guide to the creatures Collins created for the series.

Everdeen, Katniss (fictional
    character), 51–52
    in *Catching Fire*, 62, 65
    effect of violence, 10–11
    as feminist, 64
    in film, *52*, 80–82, *81*
    story told by, 52–53
Everdeen, Prim (fictional character), 52

F
Feminism, 64

G
Generation O! (television program),
    30–31
Gladiator games, 51, 77
Goodman, Alan, 29–30
Gregor (fictional character)
    adventures, 35, 36
    father of, 37
    violence and, 41, 46, 72
Gregor and the Code of Claw, 44, *45,* 46
*Gregor and the Curse of the
    Warmbloods,* 44
Gregor and the Marks of Secret, 43
Gregor the Overlander
    dramatic question, 38
    opening, 35
    popularity, 40
    publication, 40
    reviews, 40–41
    sequels, 42, 43–44, *45,* 46
    theme, 72
    use of life experiences, 35–36, 37

H
Harry Potter series, 68
Hart, Melissa Joan, *27*
Hawthorn, Gale (fictional character)
    in *Catching Fire*, 62
    effect of violence, 11
    in film, 79, *79*
Hemsworth, Liam, 79

Honors. *See* Awards and honors
The Hunger Games (book)
    audience, 55, 58
    book deal, 47
    descriptions of violence, 55
    first person voice, 52–53
    initial print run, 56–57
    inspirations, 11, *47,* 48–51, *49,*
        53–55, *54*
    popularity, 8, 58, 69–70
    reviews, 57–58
    themes, 8, 53–55
The Hunger Games (film), *83*
    casting, 78, 78–82, *79, 81*
    effect on book sales, 8
    ethical issues, 77–78
    non-writing roles, 77, 78–79
    writing, 74–77
The Hunger Games (trilogy)
    plagiarism accusation, 71
    reviews, 71–72
    sales, 68, 82
    writing, 58–60
    See also specific titles
Hutcherson, Josh, 78, *79*

I
"In Flanders Field" (McCrea), 17
Indiana University (IU) in
    Bloomington, 21–22
Interviews, 82
Isabel (fictional character), 41

J
Jacobson, Nina, 74, 75, 77–78

K
Kitt, Eartha, *32, 33*

L
Languages, learning, 21
Lawrence, Jennifer, *52,* 80–82, *81*
L'Engle, Madeline, 18

Picture Credits

Cover: © PHOTOlink.net/Maggie Wilson/newscom
© AP Images/Barbara Nitke 54
© AP Images/PRNewsFoto/Nick Jr., Nickelodeon 59
© AP Images/Victoria Will 21, 61, 67
© Ben Molyneux/Alamy 68
© Bettmann/Corbis 14
© Blue Lantern Studio/Corbis 19
© Bruce Fleming/Getty Images 32
© Carolco/The Kobal Collection /Art Resource, NY 47
© Hand-Out/Indigo Books & Music inc./Newscom 65
© HO/MCT/Newscom 45
© Jeff Malet Photography/Newscom 70
© Leon Retna Ltd/Corbis 57
© Lionsgate/Photofest 76, 79, 83
© Mary Evans Picture Library/Alamy 49
© Mirek Towski/DMI/Time Life Pictures/Getty Images 27
© MShieldsPhotos/Alamy 36
© mZUMA Press/Newscom 9
© NetPhotos/Alamy 40
© The NYC Collection/Alamy 24
© Phil Degginger/Alamy 43
© PHOTOlink.net/Maggie Wilson/newscom
© Rex Features via AP Images 52, 78, 81
© Trae Patton/NBC/NBCU Photo Bank/Getty Images 54

About the Author

Elizabeth Hoover is a writer who specializes in writing about books. She lives with her "very important" cat Sammy in Pittsburgh, Pennsylvania.